Masters of cinema

Woody Allen

Florence Colombani

Woody Allen on the set of
Oedipus Wrecks (1989).

Contents

Introduction

Who has not decided, one Sunday afternoon, to go and see 'Woody Allen's latest', ninety minutes — seldom more — of sparkling dialogue and New York glamour? In a career spanning forty years Allen has become a cultural stereotype. In the eyes of the world, Brooklyn's red-headed son is now the archetypal Manhattan intellectual, Jewish and terribly neurotic. Hence the impression that his films are like champagne bubbles, undoubtedly refined, but ultimately a bit pointless.

In reality, Allen's art is much greater than this. Comedic virtuoso and inspired tragedian, instigator of new forms and boldly inventive, as a director Allen has the elegance to clothe his undeniable depths in lightness. Too often we forget the stylistic innovations of *Annie Hall* or the perfect comic mechanism that is *Manhattan Murder Mystery*. Not that all his films have been masterpieces — Allen's cinematic proligacy has inevitably meant that his output has been somewhat uneven — but each film is another brick in the wall he is patiently building.

In one of the last sequences of *Manhattan*, Isaac records a list of the things that make life worth living: 'Ooh, I would say Groucho Marx, to name one thing, and Willie Mays, and … the second movement of the 'Jupiter' Symphony, and … Louis Armstrong's recording of 'Potato Head Blues', Swedish movies, naturally, *Sentimental Education* by Flaubert, Marlon Brando, Frank Sinatra, those incredible apples and pears by Cézanne, the crabs at Sam Wo's, Tracy's face.' Carried away by this singular epiphany, a mix of literature, gastronomy and love, Isaac leaps up and, accompanied by the majestic sounds of Gershwin's *Rhapsody in Blue*, goes at last to the girl he loves.

Most fans of Allen's films would also include Louis Armstrong on their personal list — anyone who loves Woody loves jazz … And Swedish films, because you can't like *Interiors* or *September* without being interested at some time or other in the work of Ingmar Bergman. At the bottom of their list, in gold letters, they would write 'Woody Allen'.

Diane Keaton and Woody Allen in *Annie Hall* (1977).

From Brooklyn to the Upper East Side

The young Woody Allen shoots to fame

Woody Allen in 1972.

Allan Stewart Konigsberg

Over an ordinary, rain-soaked street, with a grey ocean in the distance, comes the famous nasal voice: 'The scene is Rockaway. The time is my childhood. It's my old neighbourhood … and forgive me if I tend to romanticize the past. I mean, it wasn't always as stormy and rain-swept as this. But I remember it that way … because that was it at its most beautiful.' So opens *Radio Days* (1987), Woody Allen's film based on his childhood memories. For anyone who knows the work of New York's most famous son, the unremarkable urban landscape, with its unostentatious, melancholic beauty, will be instantly familiar. More surprising is the affectionate nostalgia apparent in the commentary. For, from his first feature, *Take the Money and Run* (1969), to his character of a writer traumatized by his early life in *Deconstructing Harry* (1997), Allen usually gives the childhood of his alter egos an atmosphere of cloying sadness, sometimes turning to deep depression.

Why? The films themselves provide an answer: he did not have a good relationship with his parents. We see this early emotional trauma in *Take the Money and Run*, where the hero's parents appear in Groucho Marx masks because, the narrator tells us, they are 'ashamed of their son's criminal record'.[1] Of this famous visual gag Allen later said drily that his parents did not deserve to have people see their faces. His biographer Eric Lax described witnessing Allen, then in his fifties, saying to his mother, 'I remember you would hit me every day when I was a child.'[2] Similarly in *Wild Man Blues* (1997), Barbara Kopple's documentary about Allen, we see his untempered adolescent hostility to his parents, then aged ninety-seven and ninety-one and he tells the director that his mother 'slapped [him] every day of [his] life'. Although *Radio Days* offers a warmer picture of the filmmaker's early life, it also shows the slaps raining down on the head of Joe (Seth Green), alias Woody as a boy. This heavy weight of emotional wounds and resentments is scathingly summed up in *Oedipus Wrecks* (1989; the section Allen directed for the portmanteau film *New York Stories*), in which the mother of Allen's character, Sheldon Millstein, floats in the sky over Manhattan telling the whole island her many grievances against her terrible son.[3] 'I love her, but I wish she would disappear', Sheldon tells his analyst.

So, the parents of Allan Stewart Konigsberg – Woody Allen's real name – are certainly present in his work. But his films reveal very little about them. We have to turn to the biographers to discover that Martin Konigsberg and Nettie Cherry were both born into practising Jewish families in the United States. Martin's father Isaac had left Russia for New York in 1899. For some time he prospered as a coffee trader, but lost everything in the crash of 1929 and turned to selling dairy products at the Wallabout Market near Brooklyn's Williamsburg docks. It was here that Isaac encountered Nettie, book-keeper for one of the market wholesalers and the daughter of an Austrian immigrant who had been in New York since 1891. Isaac quickly introduced the energetic young redhead to his favourite son, Marty. The couple married in 1931 and set up home in Brooklyn. There were tensions in the marriage from the beginning. Lack of money meant Nettie had to give up the studies she could have pursued and, stuck at home with the housework, she did not hide her bitterness. Soon she began criticizing her husband for his lack of professional ambition, holding him responsible for their financial difficulties. Their first child, Allan Stewart, was born in a Bronx hospital on 1 December 1935. In 1943 the family expanded with the birth of a daughter, Letty.

In the first seven years of Allan's life the Konigsbergs moved more than a dozen times, always remaining within Brooklyn, whose different neighbourhoods (the Konigsbergs lived mainly in Flatbush) were home to Jewish immigrants and penniless artists.[4] Wherever they lived, the Konigsbergs always had lodgers. They had one of Nettie's unmarried sisters living with them (like Aunt Bea in *Radio Days*), and a series of distant relations arrived from Europe to escape Hitler. At home, Yiddish was spoken more often than English. Mr and Mrs Konigsberg rowed a great deal and their son grew up in an anxious atmosphere of parental disputes and chronic lack of money. 'My parents never got divorced, though I begged them to', sighs Allan Felix in *Play It Again, Sam* (1972)[5] Marty Konigsberg had one casual job after another. After selling jewellery by mail order, driving a taxi, waiting tables and betting at the Saratoga Race Course, he got a permanent job at Sammy's Bowery Follies, a well-known Manhattan vaudeville theatre. In the idealized version of this unhappy childhood depicted in *Radio Days*, the

Martin and Nettie Konigsberg in the 1930s.

Opposite page: Seth Green in *Radio Days* (1987), alter ego of young Allan Stewart Konigsberg.

father is a rather attractive, gentle dreamer. He lets his son think he is a petty crook rather than admit he is just a taxi driver. According to Allen's childhood friend Elliott Mills, 'Marty was a small-time hustler. Whatever you wanted, he got. You wanted a typewriter, he got you a typewriter. Of course it had no serial number.'[6]

The magic of cinema

Allan went through periods of depression at an early age. 'My mother said I was a happy kid for my early years and then I was around five, something happened, she always felt, that made me turn sour', Allen told Lax.[7] There were no books at home, so he sought refuge in films. At the time,

Brooklyn was full of cinemas, from the Midwood and the Patio to the Kent, where Allen shot *The Purple Rose of Cairo* (1985) — another film full of childhood memories of the miraculous spell cast by the movies in an America traumatized by the Great Depression. In his book of conversations with the critic Stig Björkman, Allen recalls with delight his childhood years spent in the dark looking at the big screen: 'And I always hated the summertime, I hated the hot weather, I hated the sunshine. So I used to go into an air-conditioned movie-house. And sometimes, you know, I would go four, five, six times a week or every single day, for as much money as I could scrape together. There was always a double-feature to see. And I loved it! But in the wintertime, when there was school, it was a different matter. You could only go on the weekends. But usually I went Saturday and Sunday, and sometimes on Friday afternoon, after school.'[8] Luckily the American cinema of the 1940s had many marvels to offer this movie-hungry boy. It was the golden age of the big studios, which were turning out breathtaking pieces of film noir, irresistible comedies and captivating stars. Often accompanied by his cousin Rita, five years his senior, Allan devoured all these things without distinction. Perhaps because he was

Woody Allen's Brooklyn.

Young Woody Allen's favourite amusement park in Coney Island.

a puny, sickly child, he was particularly keen on the most virile actors who played the most macho roles: James Cagney, Gary Cooper, Alan Ladd and Humphrey Bogart. It was for the love of cinema that Allan Konigsberg, still a boy, crossed the East River to see the films on 42nd Street and set foot for the first time on Manhattan Island, of which he would later become a legendary resident.

So it is hardly surprising that Allen's films should reflect the prodigious memory of a film-lover. Going to the movies is the favourite pastime of their wealthy bourgeois protagonists. In *Annie Hall* (1977), Annie (Diane Keaton) arrives late for a screening of Ingmar Bergman's *Face to Face* and Alvy (Woody Allen) refuses to go in, even though the credits are in Swedish. One of the characters in *Crimes and Misdemeanors* (1989) is Clifford (Woody Allen), who goes to see films in the afternoons, hanging out in art-house cinemas that show Frank Tuttle's *This Gun for Hire*, Alfred Hitchcock's *Mr. and Mrs. Smith* and Curtis Bernhardt's *Happy Go Lucky* — all made while Allen was still a Brooklyn kid who spent all his time at the movies. Similarly, in *Manhattan Murder Mystery* (1993), the heroes go to see Billy Wilder's *Double Indemnity* and get caught up in a shoot-out behind the screen of a cinema

Woody Allen in 1952.

Woody Allen with Johnny Carson in *The Tonight Show* in the mid-1960s.

Following pages: Mae Questel (who plays Woody Allen's mother) and Woody Allen in *Oedipus Wrecks* (1989).

showing Orson Welles's *Lady from Shanghai*. But direct quotation is far from the only way in which Allen expresses his love of the cinema. Beyond the many, many quotations – visual gags borrowed from Charlie Chaplin or Buster Keaton, shot compositions from Bergman or Federico Fellini[9] – Allen is a past master of the homage buried in the plot, as in *Play It Again, Sam*. Allan Felix (Woody Allen) is a film-lover obsessed with Bogart in general and Michael Curtiz's *Casablanca* in particular. He finds himself caught up in the same romantic triangle as his hero and the story ends on the tarmac of an airport runway, exactly like the 1940s classic.

Much later, Allen returned to the main elements of Fellini's *8½* for *Stardust Memories* (1980) and combined the intrigues of Wilder's *Double Indemnity* and Hitchcock's *Rear Window* in *Manhattan Murder Mystery*. Ultimately, becoming a filmmaker enabled Allen to realize Peter Pan's dream and remain in the world of his childhood. 'The style of my films comes from my childhood, from my love of certain kinds of film, which gives them the scent of a different time, even though, technically, the action is set in the present day. And when I make films set in the past, for example in the 1940s, it's the 1940s the way it was shown in films rather than the real 1940s … My films come from a relationship to the world based on films rather than reality. Of course, that shows something about my childhood, something rather sad. At the time I spent a lot of time hiding from reality in the cinema, so much so that I couldn't tell the difference between the two.'[10]

When he was not shut away in a darkened cinema, young Allan, the future Woody, had another trick for escaping real life. For his tenth birthday he received a conjuring set and was instantly fascinated, developing an endless hunger for new tricks. Whenever he skipped school to go to Manhattan with his friends Elliott Mills and Mickey Rose, he always called in at the Circle Magic Shop on West 57th Street. As a teenager he even performed as a conjuror on stage. In 1952, holidaymakers staying at the Majestic Bungalow Colony in upstate New York could watch young Allan Konigsberg demonstrate his skills as a magician while they sipped their cocktails. He was not a great success but magic remained a hobby for the future filmmaker. It was also to be a hobby for Sandy, the main character in *Stardust Memories*, and plays an important part in *A Midsummer Night's Sex Comedy* (1982), *Oedipus Wrecks* and, more recently, *The Curse of the Jade Scorpion* (2001) and *Scoop* (2006).

Lastly, as *Radio Days* also shows, Allen grew up with his ear glued to the radio. After giving up the saxophone – which he found too difficult – he took up the clarinet and practised every day with a discipline that impressed his friends.

Woody Allen is born

All this left very little time for studies of a more academic kind. Allan was an average, even mediocre student. He developed a particular aversion to his own school, Midwood High, and his teachers there, who inspired the much-quoted line from *Annie Hall*: 'Those who can't do, teach, and those who can't teach, teach gym. And … uh, h'h, of course, those who couldn't do anything, I think, were assigned to our school.' During his years at Midwood, Allan Konigsberg became Woody Allen: 'Allen' because it is the usual spelling of 'Allan' and 'Woody' by 'arbitrary' choice.[11] It was under this pseudonym, soon to become his new identity, that in the spring of 1952 he began sending jokes to the New York press and was immediately published by Earl Wilson of the *New York Post*, who had no idea he was dealing with a sixteen-year-old boy. The jokes made their mark and very soon Allen became a paid collaborator of David O. Albert, a press attaché at the head of an advertising agency in charge of several stars' images. Allen's job was to make up amusing quotations and place them in newspapers, attributing them to the celebrities represented by the firm. Soon he was making $25 a week. Among his colleagues he particularly appreciated Mike Merrick and Don Garrett, two veterans of the radio who had been professional humorists for decades. After work they liked to have a beer and tell their young protégé funny stories and anecdotes. Their verve and sense of the picturesque can be seen in the ageing comedians of *Broadway Danny Rose* (1984).

In September 1953, Allen enrolled at New York University, primarily to please his parents. 'Even now, my parents would be much better if I had lived up to their dream and been a pharmacist. There's tremendous pressure where I come from – a middle-class neighbourhood – to

Harriet Andersson and Lars Ekborg in
Ingmar Bergman's *Summer with Monika* (1953).

be an optometrist or a dentist or a lawyer, and
that's what my friends have become. They exhi-
bited at an early age an ability to get along at
summer camp.'[12] But starting at NYU was to be
Allen's final concession to his parents' concerns
for normality. Having signed up to study Spanish,
English literature and film, he skipped classes and
eventually dropped out after less than two years.
In the meantime a major event had occurred in
his life: he had encountered the work of Ingmar
Bergman. Although he went to see *Summer with
Monika* out of sexual curiosity (the film had a
steamy reputation[13]), Allen came out deeply
moved. 'Wonderful', he said; it was a masterpiece
that opened the gates of the unknown world of
European cinema, which he regarded as 'so much

more mature than the American cinema' because
it was 'much more confrontational and much
more grown up'.[14]

One of the most popular comedians
on the New York scene

The films he loved were solemn and serious, but
for the moment Allen's only career ambition
was as a comedian. At the age of barely twenty
he had a chance to break into television with a
job as a scriptwriter for *The Colgate Comedy Hour* on
NBC, working in Hollywood. This was a popular
show featuring several great comedians, including Allen's childhood idol, the legendary Bob
Hope. Unfortunately, the show came off the air a
few months after his arrival in Hollywood, but no

matter — those few months in Los Angeles taught him a great deal. At first the culture shock was cruel. Part of *Annie Hall* is about the unhappiness of a New Yorker lost beneath the California sun. But then Allen met Danny Simon, the show's producer and an influential figure in the television world. And then, on impulse, brought his seventeen-year-old girlfriend, Harlene Rosen, to the Hollywood Hawaiian Motel, where the television station was paying for him to stay, and the young couple were married in a ceremony conducted by a rabbi on 15 March 1954.

With the end of his television show there was nothing to keep Allen in a city he loathed. He rushed back to Manhattan, where he and his young wife set up home. With the help of Simon, who believed in his talent, he soon found work for a range of programmes. He wrote for *Stanley*, a long-running show, and then for a real star, Sid Caesar. Born in 1922, Caesar was another New York Jew and a very popular comedian of the day, who presented several shows. He was always keen to bring fresh blood into his teams and willing to give new writers a chance. At the time, Allen was working with Larry Gelbart, a more experienced scriptwriter whose main claim to fame would be the creation of the anti-militaristic television series *MASH* in 1972. Their sketches for two special shows sponsored by Chevrolet (*Sid Caesar's Chevy Show*) found such favour that they won the prestigious Sylvania Award of 1958, along with a nomination for the Emmy Awards, television's equivalent of the Oscars. Fortified by this early success, Allen could easily have settled down and remained forever in television. In 1960 he was hired by CBS's *The Garry Moore Show* and was paid the considerable sum of $1,700 a week. But, as he revealed in the harsh portrayal of life behind the scenes of a comedy show in *Hannah and Her Sisters* (1986), it was a world Allen hated.

Around this time Allen met Jack Rollins and Charles H. Joffe, agents who worked together and represented cutting-edge talent, such as the director Mike Nichols.[15] Allen told them he wanted to do stand-up. The agents were unsure at first — this young writer didn't look like much — but agreed to take him on trial and soon became his most ardent supporters. They saw their young discovery as a triple threat to Hollywood, being at once actor, writer and director — a first since Orson Welles, as they later liked to say in interviews. For Allen's first show, Rollins and Joffe sent him to the Blue Angel, a smart club on East 55th Street, where the clients could have a drink and watch a succession of different artists. The audiences proved unenthusiastic, no doubt because Allen, as a complete beginner, confined himself to monotonously reciting pieces he had written out.

Here he learned a vital lesson: it is not enough to write funny lines on paper, you have to know how to say them. Allen proved that he did not give up easily and was quick to learn. His mentors Rollins and Joffe then chose the Duplex, an unostentatious club on Grove Street in Greenwich Village. More than once the anxiety-ridden Allen felt like abandoning the whole idea. But he kept going and, in the space of two years, had become one of the most popular comedians on the New York scene. He had understood that to make people laugh he had to use his physical presence on stage and suggest an unspoken link between his routines — in which a neurotic New York Jew met with dreadful misfortunes — and his puny appearance, with large glasses and blotchy skin. Audiences laughed far more often and a palpable affection grew for this frail little man who could wield sarcasm like no one else. A recurrent target of his sketches was his wife, 'the first Mrs Allen', presented as frigid and boring. But Allen's humour was not all autobiographical. He was highly skilled at pastiche and parody, and sometimes dipped into the absurd, a legacy from his everlasting love of the Marx Brothers. This eclecticism would, of course, reappear in his films.

While performing at the Duplex, Allen met Louise Lasser, an aspiring actress with whom he at once fell in love. Their relationship precipitated the end of his marriage to Harlene, whom he divorced in 1962. He and Lasser moved in together on Park Avenue in the Upper East Side, home to New York's élite. Allen was often away on tour, performing everywhere from Chicago to Las Vegas via Los Angeles and St Louis with ever growing success. *The New York Times* and *Newsweek* published long articles about him. The young prodigy interpreted this success in his own way and decided that the time had come to make a film.

'I had a rough marriage', by Woody Allen

I wanted to discuss my marriage or, as it was known, The Oxbow Incident. I had a rough marriage. Well, my wife was an immature woman and, that's all I can say. See if this isn't immature to you: I would be home in the bathroom, taking a bath, and my wife would walk in whenever she felt like, and sink my boats …

We used to argue and fight and finally we decided we should either take a vacation or get a divorce. We discussed it very maturely and we decided on the divorce because we felt we had a limited amount of money to spend. A vacation in Bermuda is over in two weeks but a divorce is something that you always have.

I saw myself free again, living in the Village in a bachelor apartment with a wood-burning fireplace, a shaggy rug and, on the walls, one of those Picassos by Van Gogh. Great swinging airline hostesses running amok in the apartment. I got very excited and I laid it right on the line with her. I came right to the point. I said, "Quasimodo, I want a divorce."

And she said, "Great, get the divorce."

But it turns out in New York State they have a strange law that says you can't get a divorce unless you can prove adultery. That is weird because the Ten Commandments say, "Thou shalt not commit adultery", but New York State says you have to.

This is an extract from *I Had a Rough Marriage*, recorded during a performance at Mr. Kelly's, a Chicago cabaret, in March 1964, and published in *The Illustrated Woody Allen Reader*, by Linda Sunshine (ed.), Random House, New York, 1995.

Woody Allen and Janet Margolin (who plays his first wife) in *Annie Hall* (1977).

Following pages: Woody Allen and his second wife Louise Lasser in *Bananas* (1971).

A Time to Laugh

From *Take the Money and Run*
to *Love and Death*

Woody Allen in *Bananas* (1971).

Woody Allen the scriptwriter

Allen's main problem in the mid-1960s was his considerable success. In demand across the US, on stage and on television, his life was an exhausting round of endless shows and hotel rooms. He did not particularly enjoy his daily contact with the public and sometimes, when an audience was unreceptive, would punish them by turning his back on them for his best sketches. One evening in June 1963 the agent Charles K. Feldman, a true Hollywood legend, was in the Blue Angel with a client, Warren Beatty. Beatty, who had come to prominence in 1961 in Elia Kazan's *Splendor in the Grass*, already had ambitions to be a director.[16] He was certainly keener than most to control the shape of his own career. And this well-known collector of women was particularly interested in playing a contemporary Don Juan. He felt great sympathy for 'the plight of the compulsive Don Juan. It always struck me as a pathetic and funny character, a victim of himself or society or his conquests or whatever — but a victim'.[17] Delighted by their evening at the Blue Angel, Beatty and Feldman proposed to Allen that he should write the screenplay for *What's New Pussycat?* This involved reshaping (to the point of unrecognizability) a play by the Czech writer Ladislas Bus-Fekete, to which

Feldman held the rights, into a burlesque comedy about the trials and tribulations of a seducer who, like Beatty himself, whispered the title's charming question to all the women he met.

Helped by the faithful Rollins and Joffe, Allen skilfully negotiated his contract. He was paid $35,000 to write the screenplay and guaranteed one of the leading roles. In 1964, while working on the project, Allen received an unexpected honour: he and several others from the show business world were invited to an evening at the White House by President Lyndon B. Johnson. In the same year he also recorded an album of new sketches. He wrote the script for *Pussycat* very quickly, in accordance with the requirements of the producer, Feldman, who wanted a role for his then girlfriend, French actress Capucine. Beatty regarded her a poor performer and was annoyed to see his own role shrinking with every rewrite. In the end, Feldman kicked him off the project. He also gave Allen a hard time, demanding constant changes. Later, Beatty said, 'I've often thought that one experience made Woody a producer, and me a producer, because never again did we want to lose control over something that we'd created.'[18] Allen found this period very difficult. In the hands of his producers his

21

what's up tiger Lily?

woody allen's
what's up tiger Lily?

Poster for *What's Up Tiger Lily?* (1966), a pastiche of the Japanese film *Kagi no Kagi* (1965), directed by Senkichi Taniguchi.

Opposite page: Tatsuya Mihashi in *What's Up Tiger Lily?* (1966).

parodical script full of precise echoes was reduced to an endless procession of stars. 'I felt that nobody seemed to understand what to do with the film', he said to Björkman. 'I had written what I felt was a very off-beat, uncommercial film. ... And the producers I turned it over to were the quintessential Hollywood machine. ... It's a terrible way to make movies! It's all social. It's partying.'[19]

The film is certainly a reflection of showbiz society, with an extraordinary cast list, from the very young Romy Schneider to the veteran Peter Sellers and from Jean-Luc Godard's little soldier Michel Subor to Bond girl Ursula Andress. Peter O'Toole plays the incorrigible Don Juan character originally intended for Beatty. Allen plays Viktor, best friend of the seducer, whose fiancée he is, of course, in love with. Filming enabled Allen to discover Paris, which became one of his favourite cities. But the whole *Pussycat* business left him cynical. He despised the film and, when it came out in New York, said in the press that he didn't

even want to see it. However, in commercial terms *What's New Pussycat?* was a huge hit, a box-office triumph, earning its writer a new contract. Allen was to write the English dialogue for a Japanese crime thriller, *Kagi No Kagi*, which became *What's Up Tiger Lily?* in English. At the same time, in 1966, he began writing regularly for *The New Yorker*, one of America's most prestigious weekly magazines. He published amusing stories, often pastiches of great western writers, from the existentialists to the Russian novelists. It was an exercise in which this self-taught literary latecomer proved to excel: 'I always said that I could write before I could read. … Nothing makes me happier than to tear open a big ream of yellow or white paper. And I can't wait to fill it! I love to do it.'[20] The 16 March 1968 issue published 'Notes from the Overfed', an excellent parody of Dostoevsky: 'I was having tea and cracknels with my uncle at a fine restaurant. Suddenly my uncle put a question to me. "Do you believe in God?" he asked. "And if so, what do you think He weighs?" So saying, he took a long and luxurious draw on his cigar and, in that confident,

assured manner he has cultivated, lapsed into a coughing fit so violent I thought he would hemorrhage.'[21] The course outline offers an introduction to psychology, which teaches 'the theory of human behavior': 'Why some men are called "lovely individuals" and why there are others you just want to pinch. Is there a split between mind and body, and, if so, which is better to have?' (*The New Yorker*, 29 April 1967).[22] Between 1966 and 1980 Allen wrote regularly for *The New Yorker*. The paper's head of fiction, Roger Angell, was a demanding and attentive editor who detected a regrettable lack of self-esteem in his star writer. He recalled a conversation with Allen in the following terms for the director's biographer, Marion Meade:

'I certainly hope you're not one of those writers who think humor isn't important enough for a man to be remembered for.'

'I am.'

'Writing humor is a serious business', Angell argued. 'Do you mean it's not serious enough for you?'

'I do mean that.'[23]

Daliah Lavi and Woody Allen in the section of *Casino Royale* directed by Val Guest (1967).

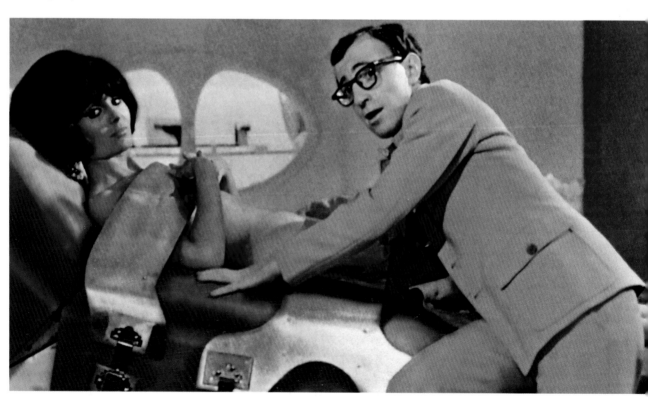

Woody Allen (left) in the 1970s and Groucho Marx (right) in 1941.

However, these pieces do reveal Allen's talent as a writer. Alert and subtle, he creates real characters, even when he is simply writing parody. Which is why *What's Up Tiger Lily?* is such a disappointment. The dialogue is certainly funny and inventive but, spoken by characters Allen inherited rather than created, it loses its flavour. His appearances (in the role of the projectionist who appears in a shadow play with his girlfriend Louise Lasser) are roughly drafted and not funny enough to save the whole. Furious with the 'insipid' *Tiger Lily*, Allen tried to block its release by attacking the producer.[24] But he was wasting his time. The film came out and was a big hit. In the meantime, on 2 February 1966, Allen married Louise Lasser, with whom he was living on East 79th Street.

The issue of control over work surfaced again with *Casino Royale*. In 1953 Charlie Feldman had shown undeniable flair in buying the rights to a novel by Ian Fleming whose hero, James Bond, was gathering enthusiastic admirers. But with a string of other projects on the go, Feldman took a while to get down to his adaptation, with the result that another producer, Albert Broccoli, bought the rights to all Fleming's other novels and produced *Dr. No* (directed by Terence Young in 1962). The rest is history. Feldman was determined to profit from the rights to *Casino Royale* come what may and decided, in the mid-1960s, to turn it into a parody. Allen was brought in for the script, along with nine other authors of repute, including Terry Southern, co-writer of Stanley

Kubrick's *Dr. Strangelove*, Ben Hecht, who worked with Alfred Hitchcock and Howard Hawks, and Billy Wilder. With ten screenwriters and five directors (including John Huston), it was hard to establish an overall structure. The end result is a strange ragbag featuring an extraordinary procession of stars, from Orson Welles to Peter Sellers, Jean-Paul Belmondo and Jacqueline Bisset. Allen — whose contribution to the script consisted of writing his own part — plays the wicked Dr. Noah, whose dastardly deeds are performed in revenge for the humiliation of being little Jimmy Bond, nephew of agent 007 played by David Niven. Dr. Noah bears Allen's hallmark, with his evil project to rid the planet of all ugly women and men taller than himself. The film was shot in London, which gave Allen the opportunity to be presented to the Queen and to make several appearances on British television. He rightly regards *Casino Royale* as 'a dreadful film experience'.[25]

Allen in the theatre

At the time the theatre seemed a safer refuge. Allen's play *Don't Drink the Water*, written in Paris during the filming of *What's New Pussycat?*, found a prestigious producer in the form of David Merrick, a Broadway personality who had put on plays by John Osborne and Jean Anouilh, as well as the musical *Hello, Dolly!* Merrick was an authoritarian who required several rewrites from Allen and endless changes to the cast. The play tells the story of a couple and their teenage daughter

25

Woody Allen and the theatre

From his time as a stand-up comedian Woody Allen retained a familiarity with the stage that reappears in his work, particularly since he has continued to write plays throughout his prolific career. The abundance of dialogue is the first, though not the only clue to the influence the theatre has had on his films. *Sleeper* (1973) contains a hilarious parody of *A Streetcar Named Desire* and Blanche DuBois' famous monologue, reinterpreted by Allen: 'I don't want real. I want magic.' In *Annie Hall* the visit to Brooklyn provides a screen adaptation of the interactions between past and present in *Death of a Salesman*. These influences are reminders that Allen arrived in Manhattan at the time the masterpieces of Tennessee Williams and Arthur Miller were being performed. *Shadows and Fog* (1991) is adapted from Allen's play *Death*, which it extends beyond the confines of the stage, with a multitude of sets and characters. Allen allows the theatre to infiltrate his more sombre films to a greater extent. Inspired by *The Cherry Orchard* and *Uncle Vanya*, *September* (1987) is like a short play by Chekhov. In his next film, *Another Woman* (1988), Marion goes into a theatre and watches a performance of her own life before the scene changes into a classic flashback. In this moment of perfect synthesis of film and theatre, the emotional realism of the first and the stylized purity of the second come together for an instant to lay the character bare.

Woody Allen with Gena Rowlands on the set of *Another Woman* (1988).

Above and right: Woody Allen and Diane Keaton
in Herbert Ross' *Play it Again, Sam* (1972).

Following pages: Woody Allen in *Take the
Money and Run* (1969).

who are flying from New York to Europe when their plane is forced to land in an East European country. They are taken for spies and have to seek refuge in the US embassy. As well as being an obvious satire on American imperialism, the play is an opportunity for Allen to deploy his wit and to put in a few leitmotifs, such as the unexpected use of magic. The play was performed at the Morosco Theatre and did very well, with a comfortable run of over 590 shows.[26] Mr and Mrs Konigsberg were very proud to see their son a playwright with his portrait in *Life* magazine and, as an ultimate sign of success, Allen's first wife, Harlene Rosen, sued him for defamation, accusing her ex-husband of tarnishing her image and ridiculing her 'at various places and times unknown to me in shows, broadcasts, in conversation and otherwise'.[27] The two sides took a long time to reach a satisfactory financial settlement. In a

letter to Allen, Groucho Marx, Allen's idol and now friend, wrote, 'For God's sake, don't have any more success—it's driving me crazy.'[28]

Take the Money and Run

In 1968, at the age of thirty-three, Allen finally became a director. *Take the Money and Run* was a long-standing project written with his childhood friend Mickey Rose,[29] and was offered to several directors, including Jerry Lewis. Feldman (who died the year the film was made) had tried for years to persuade United Artists to take a gamble on the screenplay, but in the end it was Rollins and Joffe, Allen's agents-turned-producers, who secured the necessary finance. The film is a crazy, fake documentary about a character called Virgil Starkwell, played by Allen himself, a notorious criminal who specializes in hold-ups and spectacular escapes. It makes good use of Allen's feeling for visual gags

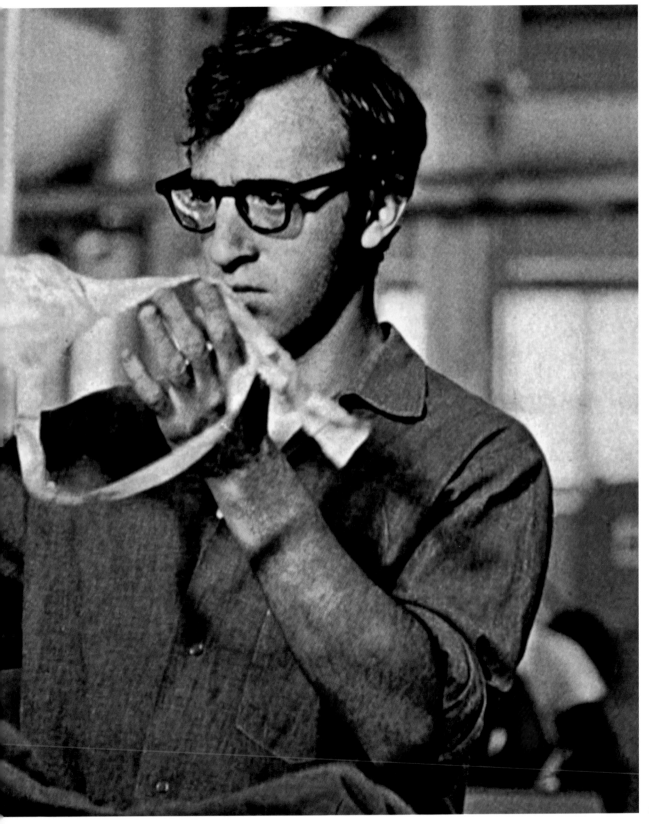

in portraying an irrepressibly bungling individual, obsessed with money and women. Of course it also uses parody and discreet borrowings: the entire relationship between Virgil and Louise, played by Janet Margolin, is directly descended from Chaplin — a variation on the relationship between a tramp and a beautiful, pure and generous soul. For the rest, the film is indebted primarily — as the masks worn by Virgil's parents indicate — to the Marx Brothers and their jubilatory version of the absurd. The most surprising aspect is Allen's visual audacity, combining archive footage with fiction, intercut with interviews with people who have known Starkwell. In its form, *Take the Money and Run* is a forerunner of Allen's later masterpiece, *Zelig* (1983). Unhappy with his initial cut, Allen brought in veteran editor Ralph Rosenblum, who revised the structure.[30]

Take the Money and Run was a hit with audiences and critics alike, enabling Allen to return to another of his great passions, the theatre. In his new play, *Play It Again, Sam*, Allan Felix falls in love with Linda, his best friend's wife, and the development of the love story is punctuated by his imaginary conversations with Humphrey Bogart. While Allen wrote the part of Allan for himself, he still had to find a Linda. In the autumn of 1968 he was at the Broadhurst Theater with a pretty and very nervous novice actress, Diane Keaton. Born in California in 1946, Keaton had come to New York to study theatre and dance. Her only claim to fame at that point in her career was appearing

fully dressed — unlike the rest of the cast — in the famous hippie musical, *Hair*. Allen's meeting with Keaton finished off his marriage to Lasser, who was suffering badly as a result of her mother's suicide and her own bipolar disorder. The couple were divorced in Mexico in 1970, but Allen did not immediately stop giving parts to his ex-wife, who appears in *Bananas* (1971) and *Everything You Always Wanted to Know About Sex* (1972). Her self-destructive personality remained fascinating to Allen, who was to reinvent it through Charlotte Rampling in *Stardust Memories* (1980), Christina Ricci in *Anything Else* (2003) and Scarlett Johansson in *Match Point* (2005). The heroine of the tragic strand of *Melinda and Melinda* (2004) combines Lasser's dominant traits as seen by Allen: an extremely attractive woman who undervalues herself, is often on the verge of hysteria and sinks into dependency on drugs and alcohol.

Bananas

Play It Again, Sam appealed to the public and coincided with a very creative period for its author, partly linked to his meeting with Keaton. At the same time, Allen's father, Martin Konigsberg, became a courier for Rollins and Joffe, who were now heading a company that was to co-produce all Allen's films until the early 2000s. Allen himself was at the peak of his popularity. He was making over $1 million a year and bought a penthouse on 5th Avenue. *Bananas* was shot mainly in Puerto Rico. Written with Mickey Rose, it is a farce based on 'Viva Vargas!', a piece originally published by Allen in the magazine *Evergreen Review*. It tells the story of how Fielding Mellish (played by Allen) falls in love with a political activist and finds himself caught up in a revolution in an imaginary Latin American republic. Built around a series of visual gags, *Bananas* refines the style of *Take the Money and Run* but makes a similar use of parody (particularly of Eisenstein's *Battleship Potemkin* and several films by Luis Buñuel). *Bananas* is short and maintains its fast pace more or less throughout. Allen's own screen persona acquires its finishing touches. The Virgil of *Take the Money and Run* was born in Baltimore and had enough nerve to hold up a bank; Fielding, like so many of the characters to come, is a New Yorker and an incorrigible coward. The film offers glimpses of Allen the cabaret performer, engaging with the contemporary world. The republic of San Marcos is highly suggestive of Cuba, with its own revolutionary-turned-dictator. At the end of *Bananas*, Fielding, who has become a star in the US, marries Nancy (Louise Lasser) and their wedding night is shown on television, with a commentary by the well-known sports broadcaster, Howard Cosell. While the film's political humour has — inevitably — dated, this ending now seems to foreshadow a society obsessed with private lives and their exposure on the small screen, which would one day peer with equally avid attention at Allen's own personal life.

Everything You Always Wanted to Know About Sex (But Were Afraid to Ask)

Allen and Keaton were no longer romantically involved after the shooting of *Bananas*, but at a professional level they were closer than ever. Watching television one evening with his future Annie Hall, Allen came upon an interview with Dr David Reuben, a Californian psychiatrist and author of *Everything You Ever Wanted to Know About Sex*, a best-selling handbook providing answers to common questions. Rollins and Joffe bought the rights to the book from Elliott Gould who, like Allen, had had the idea of turning it into a film comedy. With the addition of a sub-title (*But Were Afraid to Ask*), Allen's film, comprising seven sketches, was allocated a big budget by United Artists, the studio founded in 1919 by Charlie Chaplin, Douglas Fairbanks and Mary Pickford. In 'Why do

some women have trouble reaching an orgasm?' Allen delivers a hilarious parody of Italian films of the 1960s, copying the socialite world of Fellini's *La Dolce Vita* and the hieratic figures of films by Michelangelo Antonioni. In the now-legendary image in the final sketch, 'What happens during ejaculation?', Allen plays a sperm, but he does not appear at all in the funniest sketch, 'What is sodomy?', which tells the tender story of love between a man (the imperturbable Gene Wilder) and a sheep. *Everything You Always Wanted to Know …* was one of the ten highest earning films of 1972 in the US. In the same year a film adaptation of *Play It Again, Sam*, directed by Herbert Ross, confirmed Allen's immense popularity.

If Allen benefited from absolute artistic freedom right through to the late 1990s, it was primarily due to this series of hits. In ten years he had moved from the status of a comedian to that of a film *auteur* and writer, with a collection of his comic pieces in *The New Yorker* published in book form. Arthur Krim, president of United Artists, saw Allen as his spiritual son and gave him a contract that reduced his obligations to the minimum, effectively giving him *carte blanche* to make the films he wanted to make. This was an unheard-of luxury in the American cinema, even in the 1970s when young filmmakers like Spielberg, Scorsese and Coppola were struggling to break free of the rule of the studios.

Woody Allen on the set of *Everything You Ever Wanted to Know About Sex (But Were Afraid to Ask)* (1972).

Diane Keaton and Woody Allen in
Sleeper (1973).

Woody Allen the actor

At first sight it seems that the real Woody Allen and the one we see in his films are the same person: both wear big glasses, talk fast and punctuate their brilliant conversation with outbursts of 'Jesus!'. Does this mean Allen always plays himself? Some of the films he has made as an actor suggest this is so, particularly those directed by Paul Mazursky and Alfonso Arau, to which he simply lends his appearance and tics. And of course many of the visual gags in *A Midsummer Night's Sex Comedy* (Allen on his flying bicycle) and *Scoop* (Allen driving a Smart car) would lose their meaning with a different actor. However, unlike Chaplin's tramp, Allen's character doesn't really stay the same from one film to the next. There are at least two Woody Allens:

the neurotic, lovable intellectual (*Love and Death*,1975; *Manhattan*, 1979; *Hannah and Her Sisters*) and the seedy, vaguely pathetic crook (*Take the Money and Run*; *Small Time Crooks*, 2000). A third appears in the self-portrait films, a kind of mixture of the other two. In *Stardust Memories and Deconstructing Harry* the character Allen plays is a misanthropic artist whose weaknesses and profound cowardice are unflinchingly laid bare. The instantly recognizable mask of Woody Allen conceals a true actor, not evident so much in his range, but in the intensity of his physical incarnations. This conception of what it is to be an actor is wonderfully summed up in *Zelig* (1983), a film about the chameleon that is Woody Allen.

Woody Allen in *Zelig* (1983).

Sleeper

After his sketch film, which enabled him to try out different styles, Allen began writing *Sleeper* (1973). This time his co-writer was Marshall Brickman, another Brooklyn boy adopted by Rollins and Joffe, an unusual character who was for a while bassist for The Mamas & The Papas. Brickman and Allen wrote a carefully constructed screenplay, with a clear plot, far from just a series of gags. Miles Monroe (Allen), owner of The Happy Carrot health food restaurant in Greenwich Village, is given an anaesthetic in 1973 and wakes up in 2173. The US has become a dictatorship governed by a terrifying Big Brother. To escape from the police, Miles disguises himself as a robot. He is bought by Luna (Diane Keaton), a wealthy snob, whom he kidnaps to join the Resistance. The couple eventually manage to reveal the truth about the dictator and to overturn the regime. Aesthetically, *Sleeper* borrows from François Truffaut's *Fahrenheit 451* and Stanley Kubrick's *2001: A Space Odyssey*. It is a lively comedy that mines the differences between Allen and Keaton to the full, the lovable clumsiness of the one contrasting with the charming eccentricity of the other. Their shared vivacity also lights up Allen's next film, *Love and Death* (1975), the last of his pure comedies of the 1970s,

whose only ambition is to make people laugh. Meanwhile, *Sleeper* was a box-office hit.

By this time, Allen had established a personal routine that he was not to change for several decades. On Monday evenings he would be at Michael's Pub, where he played clarinet in his jazz band, the New Orleans Funeral and Ragtime Orchestra. Three times a week an analyst would come to his home and continue his therapy, which had already lasted fifteen years. The rest of the time he would be writing or making a film. In 1974, Allen deviated from this pattern by agreeing to act in someone else's film. One of his rare incursions into more political terrain, Martin Ritt's *The Front*, released in 1976, dealt with the McCarthyite period. This was a subject in which Allen had been interested since his meeting in 1963 with Alvah Bessie, a screenwriter-turned-theatre director and one of the group known as the Hollywood Ten.[31] In this worthy film, Allen soberly plays the part of Howard Prince, a restaurant cashier who works as a book-maker on the side to supplement his meagre income. His childhood friend Hecky (Zero Mostel), a blacklisted screenwriter, asks if he can use Prince's name. No one suspects the trick and Howard becomes a celebrated author, until all turns to tragedy.

Woody Allen and Diane Keaton in *Love and Death* (1975).

Love and Death

Allen was sole writer of *Love and Death* (1975), a film that reflects his deep knowledge of great literature. Like Tolstoy's *War and Peace*, the story is set in Russia at the time of the Napoleonic Wars. Boris Grushenko (Allen) secretly loves his cousin Sonja (Keaton), who prefers his brother Ivan. Boris goes off to war and unintentionally becomes a hero. On his return he marries Sonja, taking her off on an ill-fated expedition to assassinate Napoleon. With its sparkling dialogue, hilarious gags and nods to Bergman (Boris talks to a Death straight out of *The Seventh Seal*) and Dostoevsky, *Love and Death* is a fire-cracker of a film and the best of the period for Allen, whose skill as a director was no longer in doubt. It had a large budget and was shot in France and Hungary with an excellent, partly French crew. The delicately beautiful photography was by Ghislain Cloquet, a great cinematographer who already had several masterpieces under his belt (including Alain Resnais' *Night and Fog*, Robert Bresson's *Au hasard Balthazar* and Jacques Demy's *Les Demoiselles de Rochefort*). *Love and Death* was not as big a hit as *Sleeper*, but it did reach wide audiences both in the US and abroad.

Self-disgust was already apparent beneath the clown's costume donned by Allen for his medieval farce 'Do Aphrodisiacs Work?', the first sketch of *Everything You Always Wanted to Know …* . Perhaps because it was evidently so easy for him, Allen regarded comedy as a minor genre. In 1975 he decided to 'abandon just clowning around' and began work with Brickman on a script that was a 'first step toward maturity'.[32] The film was called *Annie Hall*.

King of Manhattan

From *Annie Hall* to *Another Woman*

Woody Allen and Diane Keaton
in *Annie Hall* (1977).

Annie Hall

Annie Hall (1977) is the portrait of a couple rather than a woman. The couple who meet and fall in, then out of, love are very similar to the one formed seven years earlier by Woody Allen and Diane Keaton. Keaton, whose real name was Diane Hall, gave Annie her own dreamy eccentricity, highly personal fashion sense and smart, uptight family. She shared Annie's taste for photography, her aspirations as a singer and even her attraction to Hollywood. When, near the end of the film, Annie leaves New York comedian Alvy Singer (Woody Allen), it is for Tony Lacey (Paul Simon), who invites her to live her dream in the California sun. Similarly, after leaving Allen, Keaton shared her life with Al Pacino and had some fine Hollywood successes, including the first two parts of Coppola's *The Godfather* and Richard Brooks's *Looking for Mr. Goodbar*. Like the actor who plays him, Alvy has two ex-wives and 'fifteen years of pyschoanalysis' behind him. His best friend Rob (Tony Roberts) emigrates to California, as did Mickey Rose, Allen's childhood friend and co-writer of his first films. In one famous scene Alvy gives Annie a lot of books 'with the word "death" in the titles'; in another he takes her to see Marcel Ophuls' *The Sorrow and the Pity*.

Woody Allen in *Annie Hall* (1977).

What does Allen have to say about his relationship with Keaton? 'I introduced her to things. I showed her films that she had not seen, that I thought were great.'[33] For her part, Keaton has said that she started therapy on Allen's advice, like Annie in the film. In other words, although the film had a brilliant co-writer, Marshall Brickman, it evidently contains elements of autobiography. These close similarities to life give *Annie Hall* an intoxicating charm, an irresistible impression that we know the characters. In their previous films, Allen had used Keaton as a counterpoint to his verbal comedy. But in *Annie Hall* he exploits all their differences. 'You're what Grammy Hall would call a real Jew', Annie says to him. Later, when he is invited to dinner by his girlfriend's very conservative family, Alvy sees himself in the eyes of the aforementioned grandmother — in the full dress of an orthodox Jew, complete with hat and side curls.

Annie Hall is striking for its freedom of tone and flexible structure, including addresses to camera, fragmented chronology, subtitles revealing

42

Diane Keaton in *Annie Hall* (1977).

the characters' secret thoughts, animation and the appearance of a dragooned Marshall McLuhan.[34] There is nothing Allen does not dare to do. Take for example the trip to Brooklyn, where the adult Alvy watches himself as a child with his family and freely comments on scenes from his past. Despite his childhood sufferings, this revisiting of his life is not without tenderness, like the film itself, which, while dwelling on its characters' neuroses, nevertheless remains exquisitely light in its seriousness.

However, giving *Annie Hall* a definitive form proved no easy task. Filming lasted almost ten months, drawn out by the perfectionism of Allen's new cinematographer, Gordon Willis, already famous for the wonderfully muted tones of *The Godfather*. The first edited version ran for two and a half hours. As with the early comedies, Ralph Rosenblum's intervention proved crucial. He chose to cut most of the scenes with Alvy's two ex-wives and refocused the story on Alvy's relationship with Annie. This gave rise to the very simple title, *Annie*

Woody Allen and Diane Keaton in *Annie Hall* (1977).

Woody Allen and Ingmar Bergman, by Eric Lax

Woody Allen discovered the films of Ingmar Bergman when he was still in high school, with the release of *Summer with Monika* (1953). He was smitten with a lifelong, leading to a primarily telephonic friendship (Allen says he only once had dinner with Bergman, during the shooting of *Manhattan*). He at first parodied (*Love and Death*) and then imitated (*Interiors*, 1978) the composition of Bergman's shots. He also borrowed the great Swedish director's cinematographer, Sven Nykvist, and his actor of choice, Max von Sydow (in *Hannah and Her Sisters*). But these are only superficial resemblances: the close-ups that are the cornerstone of Bergman's art are almost absent from the films of Allen, with his predilection for sequence shots, and while Bergman scorns music that is not justified by the action, Allen uses it to structure his narratives.

However, Allen does deal with the same kinds of themes as Bergman. The self-examination of *Wild Strawberries* inspired *Stardust Memories* and *Deconstructing Harry*; *September* (1987) is a variation on the theme of rivalry between mother and daughter seen in *Autumn Sonata*; while the whole of *Husbands and Wives* (1982) is taken up with the interview that opens *Scenes from a Marriage*. 'I think I have all the symptoms and problems that their characters are occupied with', Allen told Eric Lax; 'an obsession with death, an obsession with God or the lack of God, the question of why we are here'

This is an extract from *Woody Allen: A Biography*, Da Capo Press, New York and Cambridge, MA, 2000.

Diane Keaton, Mary Beth Hurt and Kristin Griffith in
Interiors (1978).

Hall, when Allen had been arguing since the start for *Anhedonia* (a Greek term meaning the inability to experience pleasure), to the alarm of United Artists, the distributor. The film was an instant hit. The press went into ecstasy, proclaiming it a little gem revealing a director of stature. The Oscars ceremony of 1978 was a triumph for the cast and crew of *Annie Hall*. Keaton won the award for Best Actress and Allen Best Screenplay and Best Director. The producer, Joffe, received the Oscar for Best Picture. But Allen was not present at the ceremony, which was during the night he always performed at Michael's Pub. He was increasingly avoiding interviews and the media spotlight. And he was already working on his next film, *Interiors*.

Interiors

Despite the film's bitter-sweet tone, Allen exploited his skill as a writer of one-liners in *Annie Hall*. With *Interiors* (1978), he turned his back on his past as a comedian. Influenced by both Chekhov's

Three Sisters and Bergman's *Cries and Whispers*, the film shows how three adult sisters react to their parents' divorce. The dominant figure of the mother, Eve (Geraldine Page), hovers over the film, on which she bestows her own icy stiffness. Her suicide brings the family a kind of liberation, a calm tempered with bitterness. Allen was drawing on the world of Bergman, reflected in the rigorously composed shots, extreme attention to faces, knife-sharp dialogue and existential seriousness of tone. But *Interiors* is in no way a pastiche, or an intellectual exercise based on admiration. It is a fine, serious film that does have a few weaknesses (primarily uneven performances from the female leads), but that fulfilled Allen's desire to make an 'ambitious' drama.

Allen was the sole writer of *Interiors*, drawing heavily on the difficult family background of his ex-wife Louise Lasser, whose mother committed suicide — as Eve does — after spending years in a psychiatric hospital. Louise herself inspired the character of Flyn (Kristin Griffith), who puts her pretty face about in made-for-TV movies and is hooked on cocaine. But it is her sister Joey (Mary Beth Hurt) who is most characteristic of the film. Like so many of Allen's creations — such as Lane (Mia Farrow) in *September* (1987) — Joey is a sensitive, delicate soul whose greatest suffering is that she has no artistic talent. The film portrays a family of sisters, a configuration that would become a leitmotif in Allen's work. For the first time too, Allen himself did not appear in his own film. A few days before shooting started he told *The New York Times* that he was feeling his way forward. Allen's immense artistic courage should be acknowledged here: *Annie Hall* had propelled him to the top and he was deliberately running the risk of losing everything he had struggled so hard to win. *Interiors* brought him a slough of bad reviews, admiration soon giving way to scorn. And of course the film bombed.

Interiors was a turning point, marking a move towards films of explicit artistic ambition, reflecting Allen's deeper aspirations. During the same period he also gradually stopped writing for *The New Yorker*. Three collections of the *New Yorker* pieces had been published, along with his plays.[35] That was enough. From now on Allen intended to devote himself entirely to making films. If he accepted a simple acting job during the 1980s, it was only out of admiration for Jean-Luc Godard, who suggested he should play the Fool in *King Lear*.[36] In the meantime the failure of *Interiors* left him bruised and angry with some of his collaborators, including the editor, Rosenblum, who had never liked the project. In a final upheaval, early in 1978 Arthur Krim left United Artists following a dispute with the company's owner. He founded Orion Pictures, which was ready to take on Allen, but Allen was under contract to make three more films for United Artists, though he knew that without Krim his fine artistic freedom was in danger. However, all these concerns did not prevent him from starting to develop a new project — with Marshall Brickman — entitled, simply, *Manhattan*.

Manhattan

Manhattan (1979) opens with a series of shots of the city, their spectacular beauty heightened by Gordon Willis's diaphanous black and white cinematography. In a voice-over, Isaac Davis (Woody Allen) hesitates between several openings for his new novel ('Chapter one. He adored New York City. He idolized it all out of proportion'). Soon his life is revealed, split between the intellectual, snobbish milieu embodied by Mary (Diane Keaton), a vengeful ex-wife played by Meryl Streep and a great, romantic passion for a teenage girl, Tracy (Mariel Hemingway). Built around George Gershwin's *Rhapsody in Blue*, the film offers a condensed version of Allen's world in an ambitious and often funny work that bears the stamp of his existential anxiety.[37] It became an instant classic and at least one shot, in which Keaton and Allen sit on a bench to watch the sun rise over the East River, was established as an icon of popular culture.

However, the criticisms that were to become more frequent at the time of Allen's later disgrace were already surfacing. Eyebrows were raised at the romance between a man in his forties and a seventeen-year-old nymphet. Pauline Kael, influential film critic of *The New Yorker*, wondered 'What man in his forties but Woody Allen could pass off a predilection for teenagers as a quest for true values?'[38] The reviewers were growing weary of the small world of neurotic intellectuals Allen depicted. *The New York Review of Books* published a long article by the writer Joan Didion railing against the hermetic egotism of Allen's films and their characters who went on long walks and to restaurants only to ask themselves ever more thorny questions.[39] Furthermore, some of the actors Allen worked with, disorientated by his uncommunicative approach on set, were prepared to be openly critical. Streep, for example, complained, 'I don't think Woody Allen even remembers me. I went to see *Manhattan* and I felt like I wasn't even in it.'[40] With his New York penthouse and chauffeur-driven Rolls Royce, Allen did indeed have a very different lifestyle from that of the rather penniless writers he liked to portray. At the party he gave to

Manhattan, by Gordon Willis

To coincide with the twenty-fifth anniversary of the release of Manhattan, *Tim Rhys interviewed cinematographer Gordon Willis for the American magazine,* Moviemaker *(54, spring 2004). This is an extract.*

How do you recall the *Manhattan* shoot in general – was it one of your more chaotic DP [Director of Photography] experiences or was it like clockwork?

Nothing I do is ever chaotic; I won't allow it. I think a great deal of bumping into walls and yelling comes from people getting motion confused with accomplishment. *Manhattan* was a very good shoot.

Everyone had a problem now and then, but with Woody, they were always resolved quickly and without fanfare.

Any production anecdotes that stand out in your memory?

There's the famous 'bridge' shot where Diane and Woody are sitting, talking … at first light. Well, this was shot about 5 a.m. The bridge had two sets of necklace lights, which the city has on a timer. When the light comes up, the bridge lights go off. Knowing this, we made arrangements with the city to leave the lights on. But when dawn broke … one string of lights went out. What's in the movie is a great shot … but it'll forever be with only one necklace.

Did you have any idea at all while shooting that *Manhattan* would become one of the seminal films in American cinema?

Woody and I both like black and white. It feels like New York. What we perceived this film to be was 'romantic reality', the things we both loved about New York. I've been blessed with a great string of movies … but I think *Manhattan* is still closest to my heart.

Above and opposite page:
Woody Allen and Diane Keaton
in *Manhattan* (1979).

celebrate New Year 1980 his guests included Mick Jagger, Arthur Miller, Norman Mailer, Robert De Niro and Lauren Bacall. 'What Mr. Allen says is often different with the way he really lives', wrote a disapproving Tony Schwartz in the magazine of *The New York Times*.[41]

Stardust Memories

This muted aggression and the more palpable kind he encountered in the street when he was pursued by autograph-hunting fans go some way towards explaining the atmosphere of unease in *Stardust Memories* (1980). Allen plays Sandy Bates, a filmmaker long confined to comedies, who finds the burden of celebrity hard to bear and is desperately trying to become an artist, when everyone wants him to make 'funny films'. The film combines a realistic portrayal of Sandy's daily life (the retrospective of his work at the Stardust Hotel, with crowds of fans and pretentious critics) with his personal visions. *Stardust Memories* is crucial to Allen's work, firstly because it reveals an entirely new freedom and fluidity of narration and secondly because the director reveals himself as never before. Sandy is Woody's grimacing, bitter double, a man who does not know how to love or be loved and has to take refuge in magic to escape the pain of simply being alive. This self-portrait of the artist as misanthrope did not please audiences, who shouted all the louder for 'funny films'. From *Stardust Memories* onwards it would be European audiences — won over by the success of *Manhattan* — who would continue to support Allen through thick and thin.

Top: *Stardust Memories* (1980).

Bottom: Woody Allen in *Stardust Memories* (1980).

Opposite page: Woody Allen and Charlotte Rampling in *Stardust Memories* (1980).

Woody Allen and Mia Farrow

After his break-up with Keaton, Allen had a series of brief relationships. The woman he was closest to throughout the 1970s was almost certainly his friend Jean Doumanian, whom he had met when he was touring as a stand-up comedian. It was through Doumanian that he met Bobby Zarem, an agent much in vogue at the time. And it was Zarem who, one evening in November 1979, introduced Allen to a beautiful blonde actress called Mia Farrow. At least this is one version of the story. According to another it was Michael Caine and his wife who encouraged Mia to meet the celebrated director, to whom she was attracted from afar. Born in 1945, Farrow was a child of Hollywood. Her father John Farrow — a minor director — died when she was eighteen. Before finding herself at the head of a family of seven children, Mia's mother, Maureen O'Sullivan, had her moment of glory in MGM's *Tarzan* series with Johnny Weissmuller. Mia herself was confined to bed by temporary paralysis in her childhood and, having lost her father followed by one of her brothers, had developed ways of coping with tragedy. At the age of nineteen her delicate figure and big blue eyes could be seen in the television series *Peyton Place* and she married one of the world's most famous men, Frank Sinatra. The marriage did not last, but the stir it created, followed by her dazzling performance in Roman Polanski's *Rosemary's Baby* of 1968, ensured Farrow a degree of fame. By the time she met Allen her marriage to the composer and conductor André Previn had just come to an end. She was living on the West Side of Central Park with her children: twins Matthew and Sascha, their younger brother Fletcher and three adopted orphans — Lark and Daisy, of Vietnamese origin, and Soon-Yi, a little Korean girl. Farrow's career had been in the doldrums since Jack Clayton's *The Great Gatsby* of 1974.

A Midsummer Night's Sex Comedy

Farrow's large family frightened Allen, who became her lover without ever suggesting they should live together. The couple had apartments facing each other on either side of Central Park and became a New York legend, particularly when they began working together. In 1980, Allen's contract with United Artists expired, enabling him to work with Krim at Orion Pictures. He arrived with two projects — a mock documentary about a chameleon-like man called Leonard Zelig and a variation on Shakespeare's *A Midsummer Night's Dream*. The first to be made was *A Midsummer Night's Sex Comedy* (1982), Allen's first period film since the joyful craziness of *Love and Death*. Early in the twentieth century three couples meet up for a weekend in the country, providing the pretext for a graceful lovers' dance: beautiful Ariel (Mia Farrow) has come with her future husband Leopold (1950s star José Ferrer), but allows herself to be attracted to inventor and dreamer Andrew (Woody Allen), before realizing that she really loves Maxwell (Tony Roberts). Allen and Farrow played a true couple only in *Husbands and Wives* (1992), a dark work of pain and screams. In many of the films in which they both appear, Allen's character is desperately alone in his love for Farrow's. Here the lady's favours are won by Roberts as a bright-smiling, virile and attractive WASP, similar to the character later played by Alan Alda in *Crimes and Misdemeanors* (1989).

Zelig

Allen did not enjoy shooting in the countryside, but *A Midsummer Night's Sex Comedy* turned out to be a minor hit, with a lightness of touch enhanced by Willis's cinematography. Allen's next film,

Opposite page and below: Woody Allen and Mary Steenburgen in *A Midsummer Night's Sex Comedy* (1982).

Zelig (1983), was more ambitious. Zelig 'wants so badly to be liked that he changes his personality to fit in with every group that he's with'.[42] In other words, Zelig is a chameleon: Black among Blacks, Native American among Native Americans, a goy among the goys. Allen's humour, always described as 'New York Jewish', stems from his Yiddish background crossed with the legendary sophistication of the East Coast. His Jewish roots and the ever-present threat of anti-Semitism are everywhere in his jokes. Yet *Zelig* is the first film in which Allen looks in any depth — however obliquely — at Jewish identity. 'The reference to Jewishness in Woody Allen's work indicates a more general state of abandonment by the world', wrote Jean-Michel Frodon.[43] Why does Zelig keep transforming himself? To melt into the mass, to escape eyes that might pick him out and exclude him, to take possession of a world that wants to drive him out into the margins. As a polymorphous person who can make others forget his origins whenever he chooses, Zelig is a variation on the Wandering Jew. And like the Wandering Jew, he cannot escape his tragic fate. The narrator observes that the 'Ku Klux Klan, who saw Zelig as a Jew that could turn himself into a negro and an Indian, saw him as a triple threat'; and elsewhere, 'As a boy, Leonard is frequently bullied by anti-Semites. His parents, who never take his part and blame him for everything, side with the anti-Semites.'

Broadway Danny Rose and The Purple Rose of Cairo

Zelig is also a technical *tour de force*, combining archive footage, interviews with figures such as Susan Sontag and Bruno Bettelheim, and entirely

Opposite page: Woody Allen on the set of *Zelig* (1983).

Right: Woody Allen with Charles Lindbergh in *Zelig* (1983).

Following pages: Woody Allen in Broadway *Danny Rose* (1984).

Mia Farrow in *Broadway Danny Rose* (1984).

convincing fictional scenes. Willis used 1920s equipment to obtain authentic-looking images. He and Allen stuck with black and white to shoot *Broadway Danny Rose* (1984), which drew on anecdotes from Allen's past in stand-up comedy. In the film, he plays Danny Rose, agent to mediocre comedians, who is in love with Tina (Mia Farrow), the featherbrained widow of a Mafia gangster.

This uncomplicated comedy offers a wonderful gallery of caricatures and reveals great energy from Farrow, who surprises as the beautiful airhead with a high voice. Farrow's wide range was an inspiration to Allen, who created a series of superb heroines for her over the years. In *The Purple Rose of Cairo* (1985) she plays Cecilia, a waitress in 1930s Brooklyn, who escapes her sadness by watching films. Allen put a great deal of himself into this story of overwhelming passion for the gilded, exciting, mysterious world of Depression

era cinema. Tom Baxter (Jeff Daniels), the attractive adventurer in a film Cecilia has seen five times, suddenly comes down from the screen to join her for an impossible, heart-rending romance caught between fiction and reality. The idea of physical interaction between real life and celluloid came from Buster Keaton's *Sherlock Jr.*, but the tender melancholy of *The Purple Rose of Cairo* is all Allen's own and the film is his favourite among his own works. It was much praised by the critics and, though largely passed over by American filmgoers, did very well in Europe.

Hannah and Her Sisters

In 1985 Farrow went to Texas to adopt a little girl called Dylan. Shortly afterwards, Allen suggested he too should adopt her, along with Moses, a seven-year-old boy recently arrived in the Farrow family. During this time he wrote *Hannah and Her Sisters*

Above: Stephanie Farrow and Mia Farrow
in *The Purple Rose of Cairo* (1985).

Below: *The Purple Rose of Cairo* (1985).

(1986), a group portrait in which Farrow is easy to recognize, with the love and rivalry binding her to her sisters, and her mother, a former actress who has taken to the bottle. Allen takes the role of Mickey, a comic writer convinced he has a brain tumour (inspired by one of Allen's own anxieties around the time of *Manhattan*). He also puts something of himself into the character of Elliot (Michael Caine), the unfaithful husband terrified of fatherhood. The film was shot in Farrow's apartment and the Previn children appear as extras. Even more surprisingly, Allen reworked the script during the shoot, incorporating arguments he was having with Farrow about the film itself. One of the sisters, Holly (Dianne Wiest), writes an autobiographical script that causes the entire family to recoil in horror. In drawing so openly on his own private life, Allen gives universal meaning to this warm, serious film, which has the density of a novel. It was his first film since *Love and Death* to be made without Willis, who was working on another film. His collaboration with Antonioni's legendary cinematographer Carlo Di Palma proved equally fruitful. As always in Allen's work, New York appears in all its glory and the characters are all white and live privileged lives. *Hannah and Her Sisters* was Allen's first commercial success in five years and received seven Oscar nominations.[44] But in New York, at a time of instability and racial violence, there were many who looked with irony on the sheltered world of Allen's films.

Radio Days and September

Twin to *The Purple Rose of Cairo*, *Radio Days* (1987) is an escape to an enchanted past. Like Cecilia, little Joe (Seth Green) finds his reasons to go on living in fiction. To evoke the golden age of radio in the Brooklyn of the 1940s, Allen opted to create a complex mosaic, with nearly 200 roles, intertwining amusing episodes with others more melancholic and paying particular attention to the beauty of the whole. After this, for the first time since *Interiors*, he returned to a more Bergman-like vein. Allen had reproached himself

Mia farrow, Barbara Hershey and Dianne Wiest in *Hannah and Her Sisters* (1986).

Opposite page:
Top: Seth Green, Dianne Wiest and Richard Portnow in *Radio Days* (1987).
Bottom: Dianne Wiest, Julie Kavner, Michael Tucker, Seth Green, William Magerman, Josh Mostel and Renee Lippin in *Radio Days* (1987).

Woody Allen and music

Beyond his minor talent as an instrumentalist, Woody Allen is a musical filmmaker, who thinks of his films as melodies, with rhythm and feeling. This characteristic is undoubtedly heightened by a 'trick' of editor Ralph Rosenblum, who played such a crucial part in Allen's development. 'When you edit, put a couple of records, put them on tape and – it doesn't have to be the final music for the film – throw them in behind the scenes', he told Allen (*Woody Allen on Woody Allen: In Conversation with Stig Björkman* (revised edn), Grove Press, New York, 2005, p. 34). From their opening credits, most of the films feature New Orleans jazz and Cole Porter songs, and can be described as marriages of music and image. This is certainly true of *Manhattan*, with its sublime association of black and white cinematography with George Gershwin's *Rhapsody in Blue*, or *Another Woman*, in which the heroine's grave face is accompanied by a *Gymnopédie* by Erik Satie. In *Love and Death*, the seduction scene between Allen and the countess follows the rhythm of the overture of Mozart's *Magic Flute*. In *Match Point*, the famous aria 'Una furtiva lagrima' from Donizetti's opera *L'Elisir d'Amore*, sung by Enrico Caruso, keeps returning like a portent of doom. The version is well chosen: the reedy sound of the early twentieth-century recording adds an element of anxiety to the sadness of the melody. So it is almost surprising that Allen, so skilled in using music in film, should have made only three films based on musical subjects in the course of his career: *Radio Days, Everyone Says I Love You* and *Sweet and Lowdown*.

Diane Keaton in *Radio Days* (1987).

for having provided too positive an ending for each of his characters in *Hannah and Her Sisters*. No such criticism can be made of *September* (1987), a film washed by the bitter tears of Lane (Mia Farrow), the daughter sacrificed for the career of her mother, a 1950s starlet.[45] Allen began filming with Maureen O'Sullivan (Farrow's mother), Christopher Walken and Charles Durning, but was unhappy with the result. So he granted himself a luxury unthinkable for most productions and reshot the entire film with a new cast, replacing his three leads with Elaine Stritch, Sam Waterston and Denholm Elliott. This episode clearly reveals the demanding, meticulous approach of a director who will stop at nothing to obtain the result he desires.

Another Woman

After this, when Farrow was pregnant with their son Satchel (born December 1987), came *Another*

Woman (1988), which proved a crucial film in more ways than one. For the first time, Allen worked with Ingmar Bergman's cinematographer Sven Nykvist, and the whole film shows the influence of the great Swedish director. Marion (Gena Rowlands) has just turned fifty. Through the air-conditioning vent of the office where she spends her days working on a new book, she overhears the analysis sessions of a pregnant young woman, Hope (Farrow). In this intimist film Allen creates one of his finest portraits of a woman, and an entirely new character for Rowlands, one of the most photogenic actresses in the history of American cinema.[46] He makes a complete break with the psychological realism of *Manhattan* and *Hannah and Her Sisters*. Instead of offering skilfully drawn portraits that are cruel and funny, *Another Woman* looks at the deeper pain of its heroine and is entirely played out on an inner stage.

Gena Rowlands and Gene Hackman in
Another Woman (1988).

Deconstructing Woody
From *Crimes and Misdemeanors* to *Whatever Works*

Woody Allen and Mia Farrow in
Crimes and Misdemeanors (1989).

Crimes and Misdemeanors

It is hard to imagine a more brilliant decade than Woody Allen's 1980s. Every autumn he filmed his 'Fall Project' (the title would be revealed only once the film had been cut). And every year he would present his small but faithful audience with a fascinating work. The peak came in 1989 with the release of *Crimes and Misdemeanors*, written over a summer in Europe with Mia and the children. The film acquired its structure only during editing. Halley, played by Mia Farrow, was initially a social worker and a crucial character in the film. But after rewrites and the filming of new sequences, she became a secondary character, a television producer working with Cliff (Woody Allen) on a documentary about Lester (Alan Alda), a cynical, superficial producer. Initially entitled *Brothers*, the story of *Crimes and Misdemeanors* is built around two pairs of brothers: renowned ophthalmologist Judah (Martin Landau) and his gangster brother Jack (Jerry Orbach), and rabbi Ben (Sam Waterston) and Lester. Each is faced with a moral dilemma, posed in religious terms, and discovers his own incurable solitude. For the first time, Allen brings the existentialist philosophy he read widely in his youth into contact with the religious principles inculcated into him as a boy. Judah is an agnostic, but 'there is a spark of religion from when they drive it into you as kid'.[47] As though in a tragic pendant to *Annie Hall*, Judah returns to the house he grew up in and sees himself as a boy, sitting round the table with his family. There is a discussion about whether the existence of God is conceivable after the Holocaust. *Crimes and Misdemeanors* ends in bitterness. Judah, his crime forever unpunished, goes back to a comfortable life with his loving wife; Cliff watches Halley succumb to the charms of the contemptible Lester; and it goes without saying that the rabbi's blindness is no coincidence. *Manhattan* gave us God's answer to Job in the form of Mariel Hemingway's face. Ten years later *Crimes and Misdemeanors* has nothing to warm the world, which is a pretty cold place in the view of Professor Louis Levy (Martin S. Bergmann), the intellectual about whom Cliff would like to make a documentary and who ends up killing himself.

This was a difficult period for Allen. *Crimes and Misdemeanors* came out the same year as Rob Reiner's hugely successful *When Harry Met Sally*, a romantic comedy in shameless imitation of *Annie Hall*. The success of *When Harry Met Sally* reminded Allen once again that audiences love nothing so

Anjelica Huston and Martin Landau in *Crimes and Misdemeanors* (1989).

Opposite page: William Hurt and Mia Farrow in *Alice* (1990).

much as 'funny films'. In the glossy magazines and the public's mind, he and Mia Farrow were an idyllic couple. 'Few married couples seem more married', wrote Eric Lax, whose authorized biography of Allen was published early in 1991. 'They are in almost constant communication and there is what can only be called a sweetness about them.'[48] But once the fairytale was very publicly shattered and the couple concerned began to talk, it became clear that there was nothing sweet about their relationship. Leaving aside her professional disappointments,[49] Farrow was hurt by Allen's refusal to marry her and the distance he maintained from their children (with the exception of little Dylan, who also regularly appeared in his films).

Alice

Alice (1990) was to be Allen's parting gift to Farrow. In a very luxurious Manhattan, Alice Tate lives the life of an idle bourgeois wife. An unexplained weariness drives her to Chinatown, where the good Doctor Yang (Keye Luke) prescribes magical herbs.

Like Lewis Carroll's heroine, Alice goes through many physical transformations before finally becoming herself. The film features all Allen's leitmotifs, including shifts between past and present (*Annie Hall, Crimes and Misdemeanors*), inner confrontations (*Another Woman*), a mixing of fiction and reality (*The Purple Rose of Cairo*) and the giddy freedom provided by magic (*A Midsummer Night's Sex Comedy, Oedipus Wrecks*), all in the form of a delightful comedy in which Farrow's subtle performance is given room to grow. *Alice* ends with a vision of a radiant mother, but this optimism did not reflect the filmmaker's view. On the contrary, he predicted, 'But change with a big "C", change itself, she's not going to be happy as the years go by as change happens. Her children are going to grow up and leave her and go out in the world. She's going to get older. She's not going to be happy with change. If she could have her wishes granted like an ode on a Grecian urn, she would like to freeze herself in time and stay that way. She would like to stay just where she is at a certain age.'[50]

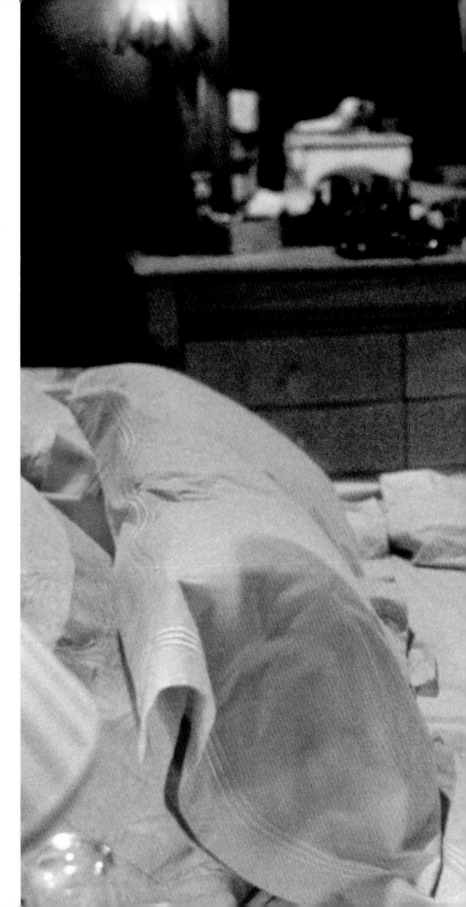

Mia Farrow in *Alice* (1990).

Woody Allen and his other actresses

Louise Lasser, Diane Keaton and Mia Farrow are the actresses most often associated with Woody Allen, because they were also his off-screen partners. However, many other actresses have contributed to his portrayal of the female soul.

Claire Bloom

The British actress made her first appearance in Allen's films in the role of the deceived wife in *Crimes and Misdemeanors*. In this film, as in *Mighty Aphrodite* (1995), the role is minimal. Was she put there primarily to score points against Philip Roth? The novelist and ex-husband of Claire Bloom has often declared his contempt for Allen.

Anjelica Huston

Following the principle later presented in *Melinda and Melinda*, she plays the same role of an overwhelming seductress twice, first in tragic mode in *Crimes and Misdemeanors*, where her lover has her killed, and again in comic mode in *Manhattan Murder Mystery*, where the wife takes fright whenever she comes near.

Judy Davis

After Judy Davis's appearance in *Alice*, Allen became fascinated by the Australian actress's expressive face. In *Husbands and Wives* (1992), *Deconstructing Harry* and *Celebrity* (1998), she takes on the classic character of the neurotic intellectual usually played by Allen himself.

Julie Kavner

Jewish and funny, this actress, whose voice will forever be that of Marge Simpson, often embodies a feminine version of Allen. *Radio Days*, where she plays the hero's mother, gave her a unique opportunity to display her talent.

Scarlett Johansson

The young darling of Hollywood first played dangerous vamps for Allen, who filmed her in *Match Point* with an obvious fascinated love. So it was very surprising to see her in *Scoop* as his alter ego, clumsiness and stuttering included. Her Cristina in *Vicky Cristina Barcelona* (2008) skilfully combines these two earlier roles, but is outstarred by an unbridled Penélope Cruz.

Dianne Wiest

Allen uses the warm sensuality of this actress as the incarnation of a reassuring femininity, in contrast to the opaque Mia Farrow (*Hannah and Her Sisters*, *September*), which makes her metamorphosis into a *femme fatale* in *Bullets Over Broadway* (1994) seem all the more striking.

Top: Claire Bloom.
Botton: Anjelica Huston.

Top: Judy Davis.
Botton: Julie Kavner.

Top: Scarlett Johansson.
Botton: Dianne Wiest.

Lily Tomlin, Jodie Foster and John Cusack in
Shadows and Fog (1991).

When shooting on *Alice* ended, Allen went into hospital, officially due to over-exhaustion, but in reality to combat acute depression. In December 1991 the adoption of Dylan and Moses was finalized after a very long process, and Allen officially became the two children's father.

Shadows and Fog and Husbands and Wives

After *Alice*, Allen agreed to act in someone else's film for the first time since his experience with Godard. *Scenes from a Mall* (1991) was a comedy with Bette Midler, produced by Disney and directed by Paul Mazursky, another Jewish actor and director from Brooklyn. Disney were secretly interested in gauging Allen's commercial potential, since his contract with Orion Pictures was coming to an end. On set, Allen behaved like a star, demanding a chauffeur-driven limousine and visits to Disney World for his children. The film turned out to be mediocre, was met with public indifference and did not lead to the offer of a contract.

His new film *Shadows and Fog* (1991) was an expressionist variation on the world of Franz Kafka,[51] shot in black and white and using musical themes by Kurt Weill to portray the nightmare night suffered by Kleinman, an ordinary man pursued by a mysterious strangler while a circus is in town. Allen brings in a handful of stars new to his world, including Madonna, Jodie Foster and John Malkovich. *Shadows and Fog* is a rather constrained stylistic exercise, a parenthesis before *Husbands and Wives* (1992), which lays its characters bare. In this film, two New York intellectuals with comfortable lives, Gabe (Woody Allen) and Judy (Mia Farrow), learn that their best friends, Sally (Judy Davis) and Jack (Sydney Pollack) have separated. They then discover the fragility of their own relationship and, while Gabe lets himself be seduced by a student, Judy falls for a fascinating man in his forties. Taking as his model Bergman's *Scenes from a Marriage*, Allen attacks the cowardice and hypocrisy of lovers with unusual violence. Most of his films make immoderate use of sequence shots, but in *Husbands and Wives* they are used systematically. The camera seems to catch the characters in passing, surprising them in the midst of arguments or when they have let their guard down. This gives the film its intensity and generates unease in the viewer, who starts to feel like a voyeur. The unease was rendered all the stronger because the film was released just as the Soon-Yi affair was publicized.

John Malkovich and Madonna in
Shadows and Fog (1991).

Opposite page: Michael Kirby in
Shadows and Fog (1991).

Soon-Yi Previn and Woody Allen in Barbara Kopple's *Wild Man Blues* (1997).

Manhattan Murder Mystery and Bullets Over Broadway

Throughout this extraordinary turmoil, of an unexpected viciousness for a man who had protected his privacy for thirty years, Allen continued to work as he had always done. In September 1992 he began shooting *Manhattan Murder Mystery* (1993), a story based on Alfred Hitchcock's *Rear Window* and first conceived of during the period of *Annie Hall*. On the new film, Allen again worked with Marshall Brickman and the muse of his early period, Diane Keaton. Whether it was the pleasure of meeting up with old friends or a keen desire to escape the chaos of his personal life we cannot tell, but *Manhattan Murder Mystery* is one

The Soon-Yi scandal

On 13 January 1992 Farrow visited Allen with their son Satchel, aged five. On the mantelpiece she found erotic photographs of her daughter Soon-Yi Previn, who was then aged eighteen.[52] It was not until August that a tabloid newspaper, the *New York Post*, revealed the affair and published photographs of Allen with his stepdaughter. At this point, Farrow and Allen were already involved in a legal battle over who should have custody of the three Allen children — Moses, Dylan and Satchel. The affair was complicated by accusations that Dylan had been sexually abused, which came from a babysitter and were relayed by Farrow. The media impact of this scandal can be compared only with that of the political sex scandal surrounding President Clinton and Monica Lewinsky in 1998. Allen agreed to appear on television, on the leading CBS show, *60 Minutes*. He said he saw Soon-Yi from time to time and rejected accusations of paedophilia. His legal action against Farrow for custody of the children lasted for six and a half weeks and ended with custody granted to Farrow. Allen obtained limited rights to visit Satchel, always in the presence of a third party. Moses did not want to see his father and the judge did not force him. Dylan meanwhile had to undergo therapy before visiting rights could be reinstated. Allen was exonerated of all charges of sexual assault on the little girl. After 1995 he stopped using his right to see Satchel. At the same time, the three children changed their first names, traumatized by the media attention.

of his finest comedies, a film of crazy charm that ends in a burst of optimism when a couple married for thirty years are suddenly as much in love as when they first met. But when it came out no one in the US wanted to hear the name of Woody Allen, who was now generally regarded as an incestuous pervert and perhaps a paedophile. His contract with TriStar was for three films, but after *Husbands and Wives* and *Manhattan Murder Mystery* the company released him from his obligations.

Bullets Over Broadway (1994) was produced by Allen's long-standing friend Jean Doumanian, who was then heading Sweetland Films, a company founded with the help of her billionaire partner, Jacqui Safra. Allen's sister, Letty Aronson, also became involved as a producer. This new situation brought considerable changes for Allen, but they are not yet apparent in *Bullets Over Broadway*, a comedy about the rich times of the New York theatre when a gangster, Cheech (Chazz Palminteri), proves himself to be a better playwright than the genius of the moment, David Shayne (John Cusack). With its delightful retro ambiance, the film is carried by a brilliant performance by Dianne Wiest as an eccentric actress and by that of Cusack, almost certainly the only actor to pull off the most difficult role of Allen's late period — the one the director would have played himself had he been younger.

Diane Keaton and Woody Allen in *Manhattan Murder Mystery* (1993).

Following pages: Dianne Wiest and John Cusack in *Bullets Over Broadway* (1994).

The lift scene
Manhattan Murder Mystery

In two minutes and three static shots, the lift scene of *Manhattan Murder Mystery* offers a remarkably condensed version of Woody Allen's comedy. Investigating the supposed death of their neighbour, Mrs House, Larry (Woody Allen) and Carole (Diane Keaton) come upon the body in a room in a seedy hotel. But in the time it takes to go and call the police, the body disappears. Larry and Carol take the lift to leave the hotel. In the first shot, which is also the longest, they have a very animated discussion. Suddenly a muffled sound tells them that the lift has got stuck.

This incident triggers the well-oiled mechanism of Allen's favourite turn as a chronically anxious character. The comic power of his monologue depends very much on what the audience knows of Allen. 'I'm a world-renowned claustrophobic!' he cries. Then, 'I'm just going to say the rosary, now', which makes us laugh because we know Allen is Jewish, and 'I'm a stallion', which is funny because of his physical weakness. As she does throughout the film, Carol takes matters in hand and starts to open the top of the lift. When she succeeds, the head and arm of Mrs House appear – the classic skeleton in the cupboard. 'Claustrophobia and a dead body. This is a neurotic's jackpot!', declares Allen/Larry, the dialogue once again showing that the scene is an exercise in variations on the well-known anxieties of a character invented several decades previously.

Diane Keaton and Woody Allen in *Manhattan Murder Mystery* (1993).

Mighty Aphrodite and *Everyone Says I Love You*

In the same period, Allen tried his hand at television for long enough to make a forgettable version of his early play, *Don't Drink the Water*. He also returned to the theatre with *Central Park West*, a one-act story of adultery similar in plot and very pessimistic tone to *Husbands and Wives*. Off-Broadway's Variety Arts Theater staged it with two other one-act plays by David Mamet and Elaine May. After stormy rehearsals, the theatre director Michael Blakemore wrote a hair-raising portrayal of the filmmaker as an asocial, paranoid tyrant. Allen had been getting bad press for some time, but the publication of Blakemore's piece in *The New Yorker*, where Allen had long published his own writing, was particularly painful.[53] Meanwhile *Mighty Aphrodite* (1995), partly filmed in Sicily, gave him a welcome escape. A Greek chorus intervenes at regular intervals to comment on the tragi-comic adventure of Lenny (Allen), who is on a quest to find the biological mother of his highly gifted adopted son. He discovers that she is a prostitute with a heart of gold called Linda. Despite Mira Sorvino's energetic portrayal of Linda and the twists and turns of the plot, *Mighty Aphrodite* is a minor comedy in which Allen's comic verve shows some signs of fatigue (particularly in his relationship with his wife, improbably played by Helena Bonham Carter).

Allen had been used to *carte blanche* from his producers, but Sweetland Films imposed countless restrictions on him. Between 1994 and 2000, producer Robert Greenhut, first assistant director Thomas Reilly, costume designer Jeffrey Kurland and editor Susan E. Morse all left the Allen ship, unable to accept Doumanian's financial constraints. All had been working with Allen for over twenty years.

Such concerns over money are far from the thoughts of the characters in *Everyone Says I Love You* (1996), a charming musical following the romantic disappointments of a family of oddballs, played out in Paris, Venice and New York. Allen's work was never so similar to the studio films that fascinated him as a child. In the glossy world of *Everyone Says I Love You* the pain of love is soothed with champagne and dinner at the Ritz. Here is all the glamour of the film in *The Purple Rose of Cairo* that captivated Cecilia so much that she wanted to enter the screen.

Opposite page: Mira Sorvino and Woody Allen in *Mighty Aphrodite* (1995).

Above: Woody Allen and Julia Roberts in
Everyone Says I Love You (1996).

Right: Helena Bonham Carter and
Woody Allen in *Mighty Aphrodite* (1995).

Opposite page: Goldie Hawn and
Woody Allen in *Everyone Says I Love You*
(1996).

Wild Man Blues

Regularly fêted in Europe, Allen was having a difficult time in his home country. After *Bullets Over Broadway*, none of his films had made more than $10 million. In a desperate effort to change his image he agreed to let the documentary maker Barbara Kopple film him on a European tour with his jazz band: twenty-three days, fourteen cities and everywhere halls packed with Woody Allen fans, come to catch a glimpse of their idol wearing his clarinettist's hat. But *Wild Man Blues* (1997) soon tires of the musical side of things. Its main character is Allen the maniac, whose demands are just about tolerated by the placid Soon-Yi Previn. In an embarrassing section, Allen notes the distance travelled by Soon-Yi from the dustbins of Seoul to their luxury hotel in Milan. And of course the Konigsbergs, now in their nineties, make a much noted appearance for yet another argument with their famous son. All in all, *Wild Man Blues* is not the PR success Allen might have hoped for, but a rather flat film in which he himself looks bored. In December 1997 Allen married Soon-Yi in Venice. Soon afterwards the couple adopted two little Korean girls, whom they named Bechet and Manzie after the jazz musicians Sidney Bechet and Manzie Johnson.

Above: Woody Allen in Barbara Kopple's *Wild Man Blues* (1997).

Opposite page: Demi Moore and Woody Allen in *Deconstructing Harry* (1997).

Sam Rockwell, Leonardo DiCaprio and
Kenneth Branagh in *Celebrity* (1998).

Opposite page: Sean Penn in
Sweet and Lowdown (1999).

Chiwetel Ejiofor and Radha Mitchell in *Melinda and Melinda* (2004).

Deconstructing Harry, Celebrity and Sweet and Lowdown

Deconstructing Harry (1997) marks Allen's return to a more sombre vein. Like *Stardust Memories*, the film is the self-portrait of an artist in crisis. This time the hero is a writer called Harry Block. With its sudden shifts in tone, discontinuous chronology, scenes from novels, nightmare visions and episode in hell, *Harry* is a fragmented, rambling film with a form as contradictory as its protagonist, 'a kind of human catastrophe'.[54] The scattered narration creates an impression of fascinating freedom, all the more destabilizing for the viewer because Harry, with his obsession with prostitutes and his destructive narcissism, is an extremely unsympathetic hero. At the end of the film, Harry thanks all the characters he has created: 'I love all of you. Really. You've given me some of the happiest moments of my life …' It is a breathtaking moment in which it seems that Allen is saying farewell to the cinema,

or at least to his previous films. Because the films that follow are a little like reunions of ghosts. *Celebrity* (1998) is an attempt to bring *Manhattan* up to date — the black and white story of a man who cannot find his place in the social circles opened up to him by his professional success as a writer and for whom redemption has the face of a very young woman. The film is crushed beneath its desire to be exhaustive and to make a full inventory of the derisory celebrities of the New York stage. Kenneth Branagh in the lead role gives a scrupulous imitation of Allen, resulting in a disembodied performance. *Sweet and Lowdown* (1999), the biography of an imaginary jazz guitarist played by Sean Penn, is based on a script written in the 1970s. Strangely, it is undoubtedly one of Allen's least musical films. Yet these films remain affecting for the beauty of their visual worlds and for some of the performances (Leonardo DiCaprio in *Celebrity*, Samantha Morton in *Sweet and Lowdown*).

Scarlett Johansson in *Match Point* (2005).

Lazy, misanthropic films

The same cannot be said of *Small Time Crooks* (2000), *The Curse of the Jade Scorpion* (2001), *Hollywood Ending* (2002), *Anything Else* (2003) and *Melinda and Melinda* (2004). The first takes its starting point (petty gangsters dig a tunnel in order to rob a bank) from a classic of Italian cinema, Mario Monicelli's *Big Deal on Madonna Street* (*I soliti ignoti*, 1958). *The Curse of the Jade Scorpion* shamelessly takes its plot from two masterpieces by Billy Wilder, *Double Indemnity* (1944) and *The Apartment* (1960), while spicing them up with Allen's favourite pastime — magic. *Anything Else* recycles characters from all Allen's films: Alvy Singer, the neurotic comedian of *Annie Hall*, reappears with the young features of Jason Biggs; Danny Rose, agent to New York's worst comedians, is reincarnated in pathetic mode; meanwhile Dorrie (Charlotte Rampling) of *Stardust Memories* returns as Amanda (Christina Ricci) — and then again as Melinda (Radha Mitchell) in *Melinda and Melinda*. This series of lazy,

misanthropic films contains plenty of jokes but lacks the mark of the great dialogue writer that Allen can be. The director changed cinematographer from one film to the next, as though he were struggling to find a collaborator on a par with Willis or Di Palma. In 2001, Allen sued Jean Doumanian and Jacqui Safra, accusing them of defrauding him of $12 million. Their great friendship was ended, along with Allen's contract with Sweetland Films. Doumanian responded by accusing Allen of fraud. The two sides reached an undisclosed settlement the following year. Allen's official producer remains his sister, Letty Aronson: 'She's family, so I know she is completely honest.'[55] After a trial run with DreamWorks, the company founded by Steven Spielberg, Allen turned to his most reliable allies, the Europeans.

Return to grace

So, *Match Point* (2005) was funded by the BBC and is set entirely in London. Like *Love and Death*, which offered a literary view of Russia; *Match Point* takes a literary view of England, heavily influenced by the novels of Graham Greene and Patricia Highsmith. Chris (Jonathan Rhys Meyers) is a poor Irishman who has decided to make a success of himself in London. He seduces Chloe (Emily Mortimer), daughter of a wealthy family, and manages to enter high society by marrying her. His sensual passion for Nola (Scarlett Johansson), his brother-in-law's girlfriend, almost causes everything to collapse. But Chris commits the perfect murder. The amorality of the ending of *Match Point* echoes that of *Crimes and Misdemeanors*.

In terms of form it was Allen's most successful film for some time and, magnificently shot by British cinematographer Remi Adefarasin, it is lit up by an amorous fascination with the young Johansson. But this fire seems already to have gone out in the next film, *Scoop* (2006), in which Johansson is no longer a *femme fatale* but a new incarnation of Allen himself, adopting his linguistic tics and mimicry. This comedy set in London is very similar to *Manhattan Murder Mystery*: a journalist comes back from the dead during a magic show and reveals to trainee journalist Sondra (Scarlett Johansson) that an attractive aristocrat is a serial killer. With Splendini the Magician (Allen himself) by her side, Sondra investigates as Diane Keaton had done before her. Between a couple of nods to Hitchcock's *Notorious* and John M. Stahl's *Leave Her to Heaven*, Allen crams in jokes about the British aristocracy and the very British insistence on driving on the left.

Staying with the British picturesque, but this time among the working classes, *Cassandra's Dream* (2007) sees two brothers agreeing to commit murder to solve their financial problems. Despite an appearance of realism in the style of Mike Leigh (who depicted a more lowly stratum of British society in his *Secrets & Lies* of 1996), this film is pure invention, film noir crossed, like *Match Point*, with a touch of Dostoevsky. The best moments come from Colin Farrell, in the role of the conscience-stricken brother. Otherwise, all the usual leitmotifs are

there: the beautiful but difficult actress that Ewan McGregor falls in love with, the irony of fate by which the brothers meet their future victim at a party, the shadow of the ancient gods (the hero's yacht is named after the prophetess Cassandra) and the nods to other filmmakers (British realist film and also a homage to René Clément's *Purple Noon* [*Plein Soleil*] at the end).

Never mind that *Scoop* and *Cassandra's Dream* seem minor films; the presentation of *Match Point* at the Cannes festival of 2005 marked a lasting return to grace for Allen, brilliantly confirmed in 2008 by *Vicky Cristina Barcelona*. Like a couple of Henry James heroines transported to modern times, two close friends, dark-haired Vicky (Rebecca Hall) and blonde Cristina (Scarlett Johansson) leave their native America to sample the corrupting charms of Europe. In Barcelona the pair are accosted by Juan Antonio (Javier Bardem), a devastatingly charming painter who makes no secret of his desire for them both. Each falls for him in her own way — chaste and tortured for Vicky, free and sensual for Cristina. The plot is thickened by the appearance of María Elena (Penélope Cruz), Juan Antonio's ex-wife and one of those irresistible neurotics that are Allen's speciality. With its delicate portrayal of a merry-go-round of lovers, this film is a return to the best of Allen's lighter vein. Its sun-soaked depiction of open, happy sensuality is reminiscent of *A Midsummer Night's Sex Comedy*: for the first time in Allen's work we see a successful ménage à trois. The film earned Penélope Cruz an Oscar for Best Supporting Actress and was so satisfying for the director that he took up his pen and let his fantasy run wild, publishing a would-be diary of the shoot in *The New York Times*. For example, the entry for 3 August reads, 'As director one is part teacher, part shrink, part father figure, guru. Is it any wonder then that as the weeks have passed, Scarlett and Penélope have both developed crushes on me? The fragile female heart. I notice poor Javier looking on enviously as the actresses bed me with their eyes … I never like mixing business with pleasure, but I may have to slake the lust of each one

Twin films?
Crimes and Misdemeanors and Match Point

Crimes and Misdemeanors is a polyphonic film in which one strand follows Judah (Martin Landau), a successful New York doctor who is unable to extricate himself from his relationship with Dolores (Anjelica Huston), a sensual, neurotic air hostess. He turns for help to his brother Jack (Jerry Orbach), a gangster who suggests murdering her. Judah agrees. At first he is filled with terror, but ultimately slips back into his quiet life. *Match Point* returns to the subject of the perfect murder. Chris (Jonathan Rhys Meyers) marries into high society, only to see his happiness threatened by his mistress Nola (Scarlett Johansson), an unbalanced actress. Like Dolores, Nola threatens to tell his wife everything. And, like Judah, Chris can see only one way out: to eliminate the problem. He commits the murder himself, with a shotgun. This crime too goes unpunished.

In depicting these adulterous relationships, Allen plays with the clichés of romantic novels: a walk on the beach in *Crimes and Misdemeanors*, an embrace in the pouring rain in *Match Point*. For a long time his heroes remain passive, as though paralysed by the tide of female neuroses (the unbearable Dolores, whose endless complaints represent an invitation to violence; the whining Chloe, obsessed with having a baby). Then comes the second phase of each film, when the protagonists take action. A word from Judah, shots from Chris – and the die is cast. From Manhattan to London, Dolores to Nola, the films echo each other, with the icy perfection of the murders they portray.

Top: *Crimes and Misdemeanors* (1989).
Bottom: *Match Point* (2005).

in turn to get the film completed. Perhaps I can give Penélope Wednesdays and Fridays, satisfying Scarlett Tuesdays and Thursdays. Like alternate-side parking.'[56]

Whatever works …

In setting up his camera in London and then in Barcelona, Allen proved that he could make films outside Manhattan. And by directing some of the most explicit scenes in his very chaste career, he won a new audience of young adults for whom *Annie Hall* and *Manhattan* are old films. Is this rejuvenated, glamorous Allen still the beloved Woody of his most faithful fans, the ones who stayed with him from *Interiors* to *Deconstructing Harry*? *Whatever Works* (2009) revealed that the answer is definitely yes. If the script of this very enjoyable comedy seems to have come straight out of the 1970s, it's because it did. Faced with the threat of a summer strike by actors in 2008, Allen had to move his annual shoot forward by three months. His new script was not yet finished, so he took an old one out of his legendary drawers crammed full of unfilmed screenplays. *Whatever Works* was originally written for New York Jewish comedian and stand-up pioneer Zero Mostel, who died in 1977. With a quick freshening-up and a voiceover reference to Barack Obama, *Whatever Works* became a 21st-century film. The lead role — of an anxious intellectual who falls for a blossoming young girl — went to Larry David, splenetic star of the sitcom *Curb Your Enthusiasm*.

Its firm setting in the period when it was written gives this film both its charm and its limitations. The charm is that of rediscovering an Allen who had been somewhat forgotten, the dialogue virtuoso and genius of the sharp, witty rejoinder. When New Yorker Boris comes into contact with religious, gun-loving embodiments of the Deep South in the shape of the family of his young wife Melody (Evan Rachel Wood), their encounters are a real joy, further heightened by the arrival of the hilarious Marietta (Patricia Clarkson), an uptight middle-class lady to whom Manhattan reveals the delights of a ménage à trois (as seen in the previous film *Vicky Cristina Barcelona*). The limitations stem from the obvious contrasts with the masterpieces of the past. There was a time — at least from *Love and Death* to *Bullets over Broadway* — when each of Allen's films was an intensely pleasurable aesthetic experience. Sadly those days are gone. Despite the involvement of the great cinematographer Harris Savides, who works regularly with Gus Van Sant, the cinematography of *Whatever Works* is very flat, without the slightest concern for lighting or set. Boris lives in the Lower East Side, a neighbourhood merging increasingly into Chinatown, but this exoticism does not inspire Allen at all; he seems to have lost all interest in the city of New York. Meanwhile the plot remains faithful to the director's grand themes: the absurdity of human existence, the constant temptation of suicide and the hope of happiness in the form of a very young woman. Allen's detractors will take cruel pleasure in noting this circularity, which sometimes gives the impression of a closed world, unrelated to the world outside. Conversely, for those who love his work, there is a particular pleasure in the annual encounter with his obsessions, manias and inimitable talent. It's no secret that Allen's life is full of rituals. Every Monday he plays clarinet at the café Carlyle. At Christmas he is in Paris, in his suite at the Ritz. And every year he releases a film (*You Will Meet a Tall Dark Stranger* in 2010, *Midnight in Paris* in 2011). So we can bet the conjuror has a few more tricks up his sleeve.

Top: Rebecca Hall, Patricia Clarkson and Scarlett Johansson in *Vicky Cristina Barcelona* (2008).

Centre: Conleth Hill and Patricia Clarkson in *Whatever Works* (2009).

Bottom: Naomi Watts, Roger Aschton-Griffiths and Gemma Jones in *You Will Meet a Tall Dark Stranger* (2010).

Chronology

1935

1 December
Allan Stewart Konigsberg is born in New York.

1943

Birth of his younger sister, Letty, who would become his producer.

1946–53

Schooling. Meeting with Mickey Rose, who would be his first co-writer.

1952

Adoption of the pseudonym Woody Allen. He writes amusing stories under this name for the columnists of the *Mirror* and the *New York Post*.

1953–5

Uncompleted studies at New York University. During this period, Allen works for several television shows and publishes satirical articles. In 1954 he marries Harlene Rosen.

1955–6

Co-writer with Danny Simon for *The Colgate Comedy Hour* and then the sitcom *Stanley*.

1957

Allen begins four years of work on *The Garry Moore Show*.

1958

Meets Jack Rollins and Charles H. Joffe, who become his agents and then his producers. Co-writer with Larry Gelbart on *Sid Caesar's Chevy Show*, which gains its authors a nomination at the Emmy awards.

1960

Becomes scriptwriter for *The Garry Moore Show*.

1961–4

Stand-up shows at the Duplex and then the Blue Angel and the Bitter End in Greenwich Village. Regularly invited to appear on television, particularly on the very popular *The Tonight Show Starring Johnny Carson*. Release of *Woody Allen*, a record of his stand-up show. Divorces Harlene Rosen in 1962.

1965

What's New Pussycat? (writer, actor). Release of record *Woody Allen, volume 2*. Publication of pieces in many magazines, including the prestigious *New Yorker*.

1966

What's Up Tiger Lily? (writer, narrator). Play *Don't Drink the Water* performed in New York. Shows at Caesar's Palace, Las Vegas. Marries Louise Lasser.

1967

Casino Royale (co-writer, actor in the section directed by Val Guest). Harlene Rosen sues him for defamation.

1968

Writes and presents a television show on NBC. Release of record, *The Third Woody Allen Album*.

1969

Film adaptation of *Don't Drink the Water*. *Take the Money and Run* (director, co-writer, actor). *Play It Again, Sam* performed in New York. Partnered on stage by Diane Keaton, who becomes his partner in life.

1970

Writes and presents a television show on NBC. Divorces Louise Lasser.

1971

Bananas (director, co-writer, actor) is the first of a long series of Woody Allen's films to be produced by United Artists. Performs as a clarinettist in New York with the New Orleans Funeral and Ragtime Orchestra. Publishes pieces in *Esquire*. Breaks up with Diane Keaton.

1972

Play It Again, Sam (writer, actor). Directs the sketch film *Everything You Always Wanted to Know About Sex (But Were Afraid to Ask)*, in which he also acts.

1973

Sleeper (director, co-writer, actor) is its director's biggest commercial success to date.

1975

Love and Death (director, writer, actor).

1976

Co-produces and acts in Martin Ritt's *The Front*. Publishes *Without Feathers*, a collection of written pieces.

1977

Annie Hall (director, co-writer, actor). The film is a popular and critical success and wins four Oscars.

1978

Interiors (director, writer).

1979

Manhattan (director, co-writer, actor). Publishes *Getting Even*, a collection of written pieces.

1980

Stardust Memories (director, writer, actor). Meets Mia Farrow, who becomes his partner (although the couple never live together under the same roof).

1981

Play *The Floating Light Bulb* performed in New York.

1982

A Midsummer Night's Sex Comedy (director, writer, actor).

1983

Zelig (director, writer, actor).

1984

Broadway Danny Rose (director, writer, actor).

Woody Allen and Diane Keaton in *Annie Hall* (1977).

Martin and Nettie Konigsberg in the 1930s.

Woody Allen in 1952.

Woody Allen on the set of *Oedipus Wrecks* (1989).

Woody Allen and Mia Farrow on the set of *The Purple Rose of Cairo* (1985).

1985

The Purple Rose of Cairo (director, writer, actor). Mia Farrow adopts her daughter Dylan. Woody Allen begins a process to adopt Dylan and Moses, one of Mia's sons.

1986

Hannah and Her Sisters (director, writer, actor). The film wins three Oscars.

1987

Radio Days (director, writer, narrator). *September* (director, writer). Making of Jean-Luc Godard's never-released *King Lear*, in which Allen plays the Fool. Birth of Satchel, son of Allen and Farrow.

1988

Another Woman (director, writer).

1989.

Allen writes the section entitled *Oedipus Wrecks* for the group film *New York Stories* (director, writer, actor). *Crimes and Misdemeanors* (director, writer, actor).

1990

Alice (director, writer).

1991

Shadows and Fog (director, writer, actor). He acts in *Scenes from a Mall* and makes television commercials for the Italian Co-op supermarket chain. Publication of his authorized biography by Eric Lax. Successfully adopts Moses and Dylan.

1992

Husbands and Wives (director, writer, actor). During filming, Farrow discovers Allen's relationship with one of her daughters, Soon-Yi Previn. The affair becomes public and features in the tabloid press for months. Start of a complex legal case for custody of the couple's three children: Satchel, Moses and Dylan.

1993

Manhattan Murder Mystery (director, co-writer, actor). Allen loses custody of Satchel, Moses and Dylan. He is cleared of accusations of sexual abuse against Dylan.

1994

Bullets Over Broadway (director, co-writer), Allen's first film to be produced by Sweetland Films, the company headed by Jean Doumanian and Jacqui Safra. He makes a television adaptation of *Don't Drink the Water.*

1995

Mighty Aphrodite (director, writer, actor). This and his five subsequent films are distributed by Miramax. Allen's play *Central Park West* is performed in New York. He acts in *The Sunshine Boys*, a television film shown on CBS.

1996

Everyone Says I Love You (director, writer, actor).

1997

Deconstructing Harry (director, writer, actor). Allen receives a Golden Lion for lifetime achievement at the Venice Film Festival. Release of *Wild Man Blues*, a documentary by Barbara Kopple on the European tour of the New Orleans Jazz Band, in which Allen plays clarinet. The Directors Guild of America awards him the prestigious D. W. Griffith Award. Marries Soon-Yi Previn.

1998

Celebrity (director, writer). Voices one of the characters in *Antz*, first animation from the DreamWorks studio.

1999

Sweet and Lowdown (director, writer). Allen appears in the films *The Impostors and Company Man*. The Allens adopt a Korean girl and name her Bechet Dumaine.

2000

Small Time Crooks (director, writer). Allen acts in Alfonso Arau's *Picking Up the Pieces*. The Allens adopt another little girl, who they name Manzie Tio.

2001

The Curse of the Jade Scorpion (director, writer, actor). In May, Allen sues Jean Doumanian and Jacqui Safra, accusing them of having defrauded him of $12 million for films produced by their company, Sweetland Films. The two sides settle in 2002. Just after 11 September, Allen releases a short, *Sounds from a Town I Love*, for an evening of television fundraising for the families of victims of the attacks on New York and Washington, DC.

2005

Match Point (director, writer), the first of his films to be entirely financed and made in Europe.

2010

You Will Meet a Tall Dark Stranger, 46th Woody Allen's film is shown out of competition at the Cannes Film Festival.

Woody Allen with Soon-Yi Previn at the 2002 Cannes Film Festival.

Woody Allen on the set of *Celebrity* (1998).

Tiffani Thiessen, Woody Allen, Debra Messing at the 2002 Cannes Film Festival.

Woody Allen in Barbara Kopple's *Wild Man Blues* (1997).

The three directors of *New York Stories* (1989): Francis Ford Coppola, Woody Allen and Martin Scorsese.

Woody Allen and Scarlett Johansson in *Scoop* (2006).

Filmography

ACTOR ONLY

What's New Pussycat? 1965
by Clive Donner
Casino Royale 1967
by John Huston, Kenneth Hughes, Robert Parrish, Joe McGrath, Val Guest
Play It Again, Sam 1972
by Herbert Ross
The Front 1976
by Martin Ritt
Meetin' WA 1986
by Jean-Luc Godard
King Lear 1987
by Jean-Luc Godard
Scenes from a Mall 1991
by Paul Mazursky
The Sunshine Boys 1995
by John Erman
Wild Man Blues 1997
by Barbara Kopple
Antz 1998
by Eric Darnell and Tim Johnson
The Impostors 1998
by Stanley Tucci
Company Man 2000
by Peter Askin, Douglas McGrath
CyberWorld 2000
by Colin Davies and Elaine Despins
Picking Up the Pieces 2000
by Alfonso Arau

SHORT FILM

Oedipus Wrecks 1989
Format 35mm. **Running time** 40 mins. With Woody Allen, Mae Questel, Mia Farrow, Julie Kavner.
• A clumsy magician puts Sheldon's mother into the sky over Manhattan, from where she criticizes him for any reason that comes into her head. The third section of *New York Stories*, directed by Woody Allen, Martin Scorsese and Francis Ford Coppola.

FEATURE FILMS

What's Up, Tiger Lily? 1966
Co-director Senkichi Taniguchi. **Screenplay** Woody Allen, Julie Bennett, Frank Buxton, Louise Lasser, Len Maxwell, Mickey Rose, Bryan Wilson. **Cinematography** Kazuo Yamada. **Editing** Richard Krown. **Producer** Woody Allen for Benedict Pictures Corp. / Toho. **Running time** 1h 20. With Tatsuya Mihashi (Phil Moscowitz), Akiko Wakabayashi (Suki Yaki), Mie Hama (Teri Yaki), Woody Allen (himself), The Lovin' Spoonful (themselves).
• The misadventures of secret agent Phil Moskowitz.

Take the Money and Run 1969
Screenplay Woody Allen and Mickey Rose. **Cinematography** Lester Shorr. **Editing** Paul Jordan, Ron Kalish. **Producers** Sidney Glazier, Charles H. Joffe and Jack Grossberg (Palomar Pictures International). **Running time** 1h 25. With Woody Allen (Virgil Starkwell), Janet Margolin (Louise), Marcel Hillaire (Fritz), Jacquelyne Hyde (Miss Blair), Lonny Chapman (Jake).
• The story of Virgil Starkwell, an incorrigible hoodlum, as told by those close to him.

Bananas 1971
Screenplay Woody Allen and Mickey Rose. **Cinematography** Andrew M. Costikyan. **Editing** Ralph Rosenblum, Ron Kalish. **Producers** Charles H. Joffe, Jack Grossberg and Ralph Rosenblum (Rollins & Joffe Productions, United Artists). **Running time** 1h 21. With Woody Allen (Fielding Mellish), Louise Lasser (Nancy), Carlos Montalbán (Vargas), Jacobo Morales (Esposito), Natividad Abascal (Yolanda), Howard Cosell (himself).
• The adventures of Fielding Mellish in the republic of San Marcos after a military coup.

Everything You Always Wanted to Know About Sex (But Were Afraid to Ask) 1972
Screenplay Woody Allen, from the book by Dr David Reuben. **Cinematography** David M. Walsh. **Editing** Eric Albertson. **Producers** Charles H. Joffe and Jack Grossberg (Jack Rollins & Charles H. Joffe Productions), Jack Brodsky (Brodsky-Gould Productions). **Running time** 1h 27. With Woody Allen (The Fool, Fabrizio, Viktor, a sperm), John Carradine (Dr. Bernado), Lou Jacobi (Sam), Louise Lasser (Gina), Anthony Quayle (the King), Gene Wilder (Dr. Ross).
• Seven sketches offering funny answers to the questions posed in a sex manual, including 'Do Aphrodisiacs Work?' and 'What is Sodomy?'.

Sleeper 1973
Screenplay Woody Allen and Marshall Brickman. **Cinematography** David M. Walsh. **Editing** Ralph Rosenblum. **Producers** Charles H. Joffe, Jack Grossberg, Marshall Brickman and Ralph Rosenblum (Jack Rollins & Charles H. Joffe Productions). **Running time** 1h 28. With Woody Allen (Miles Monroe), Diane Keaton (Luna), John Beck (Erno), Mary Gregory (Dr. Melik).
• The discovery of the future by Miles Monroe, who wakes up in 2173 after a minor operation carried out in the 1970s.

Love and Death 1975
Screenplay Woody Allen. **Cinematography** Ghislain Cloquet. **Editing** Ralph Rosenblum. **Producers** Martin Poll, Charles H. Joffe and Fred T. Gallo (Jack Rollins & Charles H. Joffe Productions). **Running time** 1h 25. With Woody Allen (Boris Grushenko), Diane Keaton (Sonja), Harold Gould (Anton Inbedkov), Jessica Harper (Natasha), Olga Georges-Picot (Countess Alexandrovna).
• Disgusted by the French invasion,

Boris Grushenko tries to assassinate Napoleon, but things go awry.

Annie Hall 1977
Screenplay Woody Allen and Marshall Brickman. **Cinematography** Gordon Willis. **Editing** Ralph Rosenblum. **Producers** Robert Greenhut and Charles H. Joffe (Jack Rollins & Charles H. Joffe Productions). **Running time** 1h 33. With Woody Allen (Alvy Singer), Diane Keaton (Annie Hall), Tony Roberts (Rob), Carol Kane (Allison), Paul Simon (Tony Lacey), Janet Margolin (Robin), Shelley Duvall (the Journalist), Christopher Walken (Duane Hall).
• The story of a romance between New York comedian Alvy Singer and Annie Hall, an aspiring singer.

Interiors 1978
Screenplay Woody Allen. **Cinematography** Gordon Willis. **Editing** Ralph Rosenblum. **Producers** Robert Greenhut, Charles H. Joffe and Jack Rollins (Jack Rollins & Charles H. Joffe Productions, Creative Management Associates). **Running time** 1h 31. With Kristin Griffith (Flyn), Mary Beth Hurt (Joey), Diane Keaton (Renata), Geraldine Page (Eve), Maureen Stapleton (Pearl), Sam Waterston (Mike).
• Three adult sisters deal with their parents' painful separation.

Manhattan 1979
Screenplay Woody Allen and Marshall Brickman. **Cinematography** Gordon Willis **Editing** Susan E. Morse. **Producers** Robert Greenhut and Charles H. Joffe (Jack Rollins & Charles H. Joffe Productions). **Running time** 1h 36. With Woody Allen (Isaac Davis), Diane Keaton (Mary Wilke), Michael Murphy (Yale), Mariel Hemingway (Tracy), Meryl Streep (Jill), Anne Byrne (Emily).
• A brilliant writer's love affairs with women and with his home city of New York.

Stardust Memories **1980**
Screenplay Woody Allen. **Cinematography** Gordon Willis. **Editing** Susan E. Morse. **Producers** Jack Rollins, Charles H. Joffe and Robert Greenhut (Jack Rollins & Charles H. Joffe Productions). **Running time** 1h 29. With Woody Allen (Sandy Bates), Charlotte Rampling (Dorrie), Jessica Harper (Daisy), Marie-Christine Barrault (Isobel), Tony Roberts (Tony). A successful filmmaker's crisis of creativity.

A Midsummer Night's Sex Comedy **1982**
Screenplay Woody Allen. **Cinematography** Gordon Willis. **Editing** Susan E. Morse. **Producers** Robert Greenhut and Charles H. Joffe (Jack Rollins & Charles H. Joffe Productions). **Running time** 1h 27. With Woody Allen (Andrew), Mia Farrow (Ariel), José Ferrer (Leopold), Julie Hagerty (Dulcy), Tony Roberts (Maxwell), Mary Steenburgen (Adrian).
• Early in the twentieth century a trip to the country gives rise to romantic complications.

Zelig **1983**
Screenplay Woody Allen. **Cinematography** Gordon Willis. **Editing** Susan E. Morse. **Producers** Robert Greenhut and Charles H. Joffe (Jack Rollins & Charles H. Joffe Productions). **Running time** 1h 20. With Woody Allen (Leonard Zelig), Mia Farrow (Eudora Fletcher) and, as themselves, Susan Sontag, Saul Bellow, Bruno Bettelheim.
• The documentary-style story of Leonard Zelig, a chameleon of a man, whose life spanned the twentieth century.

Broadway Danny Rose **1984**
Screenplay Woody Allen. **Cinematography** Gordon Willis. **Editing** Susan E. Morse. **Producers** Robert Greenhut and Charles H. Joffe (Jack Rollins & Charles H. Joffe Productions). **Running time** 1h 25. With Woody Allen (Danny Rose), Mia Farrow (Tina Vitale), Nick Apollo Forte (Lou Canova) and, as themselves, Milton Berle, Will Jordan, Sandy Baron, Jack Rollins, Morty Gunty.
• The story of Danny Rose, Broadway impresario, and his entanglements with the Mafia.

The Purple Rose of Cairo **1985**
Screenplay Woody Allen. **Cinematography** Gordon Willis. **Editing** Susan E. Morse. **Producers** Robert Greenhut and Charles H. Joffe (Jack Rollins & Charles H. Joffe Productions). **Running time** 1h 21. With Mia Farrow (Cecilia), Stephanie Farrow (Cecilia's sister), Jeff Daniels (Tom Baxter), Danny Aiello (Monk).
• During the Great Depression, Cecilia escapes her melancholy by going to the cinema – until the day the star comes down from the screen to declare his love.

Hannah and Her Sisters **1986**
Screenplay Woody Allen. **Cinematography** Carlo Di Palma. **Editing** Susan E. Morse. **Producers** Robert Greenhut, Jack Rollins and Charles H. Joffe (Jack Rollins & Charles H. Joffe Productions). **Running time** 1h 46. With Woody Allen (Mickey), Michael Caine (Elliot), Mia Farrow (Hannah), Barbara Hershey (Lee), Dianne Wiest (Holly), Maureen O'Sullivan (Hannah's mother), Lloyd Nolan (Hannah's father), Max von Sydow (Frederick), Carrie Fisher (April).
• The lives and loves of three New York sisters become entwined with the passage of the seasons and Thanksgivings.

Radio Days **1987**
Screenplay Woody Allen. **Cinematography** Carlo Di Palma. **Editing** Susan E. Morse. **Producers** Robert Greenhut, Jack Rollins and Charles H. Joffe (Jack Rollins & Charles H. Joffe Productions). **Running time** 1h 28. With Seth Green (Joe), Julie Kavner (his mother), Michael Tucker (his father), Dianne Wiest (Aunt Bea), Mia Farrow (Sally White), Danny Aiello (Rocco), Tony Roberts, Diane Keaton, Wallace Shawn.
• Childhood memories told by a narrator (Woody Allen's voice): Brooklyn in the 1940s, a time of the magic of radio.

September **1987**
Screenplay Woody Allen. **Cinematography** Carlo Di Palma. **Editing** Susan E. Morse. **Producers** Robert Greenhut, Jack Rollins and Charles H. Joffe (Jack Rollins & Charles H. Joffe Productions). **Running time** 1h 22. With Denholm Elliott (Howard), Mia Farrow (Lane), Elaine Stritch (Diane), Dianne Wiest (Stephanie), Sam Waterston (Peter), Jack Warden (Lloyd).
• Over a single summer an unhappy young woman confronts her mother, an ageing star.

Another Woman **1988**
Screenplay Woody Allen. **Cinematography** Sven Nykvist. **Editing** Susan E. Morse. **Producers** Robert Greenhut, Jack Rollins and Charles H. Joffe (Jack Rollins & Charles H. Joffe Productions). **Running time** 1h 20. With Gena Rowlands (Marion Post), Mia Farrow (Hope), Gene Hackman (Larry), Ian Holm (Ken Post), John Houseman (Marion's father).
• Marion overhears the consultations of her psychoanalyst neighbour and, through one of the patients, rediscovers a buried part of herself.

Crimes and Misdemeanors **1989**
Screenplay Woody Allen. **Cinematography** Sven Nykvist. **Editing** Susan E. Morse. **Producers** Robert Greenhut, Jack Rollins and Charles H. Joffe (Jack Rollins & Charles H. Joffe Productions). **Running time** 1h 44. With Martin Landau (Judah Rosenthal), Anjelica Huston (Dolores Paley), Claire Bloom (Miriam Rosenthal), Sam Waterston (Ben Rosenthal), Woody Allen (Cliff Stern), Mia Farrow (Halley Reed), Alan Alda (Lester Rosenthal), Jerry Orbach (Jack Rosenthal).
• A group of brothers face life's great moral dilemmas in the form of adultery and murder.

Alice **1990**
Screenplay Woody Allen. **Cinematography** Carlo Di Palma. **Editing** Susan E. Morse. **Producers** Robert Greenhut, Jack Rollins and Charles H. Joffe (Jack Rollins & Charles H. Joffe Productions). **Running time** 1h 49. With Mia Farrow (Alice Tate), Alec Baldwin (Ed), William Hurt (Doug Tate), Joe Mantegna (Joe Ruffalo), Blythe Danner (Dorothy), Judy Davis (Vicki), Cybill Shepherd (Nancy Brill), Julie Kavner (the Decorator), Keye Luke (Dr. Yang), James Toback (the Professor).
• A wealthy woman shakes off her inhibitions by means of the magical herbs of good Doctor Yang.

Shadows and Fog **1991**
Screenplay Woody Allen. **Cinematography** Carlo Di Palma. **Editing** Susan E. Morse. **Producers** Robert Greenhut, Jack Rollins and Charles H. Joffe (Jack Rollins & Charles H. Joffe Productions). **Running time** 1h 26. With Woody Allen (Kleinman), Mia Farrow (Irmy), John Malkovich (the Clown), Madonna (Marie), Jodie Foster and Lily Tomlin (Prostitutes), John Cusack, Wallace Shawn, Philip Bosco.
• Kleinman's Kafkaesque nightmare, in which he is told to find a strangler who is terrorizing the region while a circus is in town.

Husbands and Wives   1992
Screenplay Woody Allen. **Cinematography** Carlo Di Palma. **Editing** Susan E. Morse. **Producers** Robert Greenhut, Jack Rollins and Charles H. Joffe (Jack Rollins & Charles H. Joffe Productions). **Running time** 1h 47. With Woody Allen (Gabe Roth), Mia Farrow (Judy Roth), Juliette Lewis (Rain), Liam Neeson (Michael Gates), Sydney Pollack (Jack), Judy Davis (Sally).
• Two couples face the turmoil of adultery and the temptation to break up.

Manhattan Murder Mystery   1993
Screenplay Woody Allen and Marshall Brickman. **Cinematography** Carlo Di Palma. **Editing** Susan E. Morse. **Producers** Robert Greenhut, Jack Rollins and Charles H. Joffe (Jack Rollins & Charles H. Joffe Productions). **Running time** 1h 48. With Woody Allen (Larry Lipton), Diane Keaton (Carol Lipton), Jerry Adler (Paul House), Lynne Cohen (Lillian House), Alan Alda (Ted), Anjelica Huston (Marcia Fox), Ron Rifkin (Sy).
• Carol suspects her neighbour of killing his wife and begins a crazy investigation, which has the added effect of revitalizing her relationship with her husband.

Bullets Over Broadway 1994
Screenplay Woody Allen and Douglas McGrath. **Cinematography** Carlo Di Palma. **Editing** Susan E. Morse. **Producers** Robert Greenhut, Helen Robin, Jean Doumanian, J. E. Beaucaire, Letty Aronson (Sweetland Films), Jack Rollins and Charles H. Joffe (Jack Rollins & Charles H. Joffe Productions). **Running time** 1h 39. With John Cusack (David Shayne), Jennifer Tilly (Olive Neal), Chazz Palminteri (Cheech), Joe Viterelli (Nick Valenti), Dianne Wiest (Helen Sinclair), Jack Warden (Julian Marx).

• In the 1930s a young playwright manages to stage his play on Broadway using Mafia money. Along the way he discovers that gangsters can be very talented.

Mighty Aphrodite   1995
Screenplay Woody Allen. **Cinematography** Carlo Di Palma. **Editing** Susan E. Morse. **Producers** Robert Greenhut, Helen Robin, Jean Doumanian, J. E. Beaucaire, Letty Aronson (Sweetland Films), Jack Rollins and Charles H. Joffe (Jack Rollins & Charles H. Joffe Productions). **Running time** 1h 35. With Woody Allen (Lenny Weinrib), Mira Sorvino (Linda Ash, Judy Cam), Helena Bonham Carter (Amanda Weinrib), Danielle Ferland (Cassandra), Jeffrey Kurland (Oedipus), Michael Rapaport (Kevin).
• Fascinated by his adopted son, Lenny decides to find his biological mother. This is how he meets Linda, a prostitute whom he decides to educate. A Greek chorus provides a commentary on the action.

Everyone Says I Love You   1996
Screenplay Woody Allen. **Cinematography** Carlo Di Palma. **Editing** Susan E. Morse. **Producers** Robert Greenhut, Helen Robin, Jean Doumanian, J. E. Beaucaire, Letty Aronson (Sweetland Films), Jack Rollins and Charles H. Joffe (Jack Rollins & Charles H. Joffe Productions). **Running time** 1h 41. With Woody Allen (Joe), Goldie Hawn (Steffi), Edward Norton (Holden), Drew Barrymore (Skylar), Julia Roberts (Von), Barbara Hollander (Claire), Natalie Portman (Laura), Alan Alda (Bob), Tim Roth (Charles Ferry).
• A musical set in Paris and Venice portraying the love affairs of a handful of New Yorkers.

Deconstructing Harry   1997
Screenplay Woody Allen. **Cinematography** Carlo Di Palma. **Editing** Susan E. Morse. **Producers** Jean Doumanian, J. E. Beaucaire, Richard Brick, Letty Aronson (Sweetland Films), Jack Rollins and Charles H. Joffe (Rollins & Joffe Productions). **Running time** 1h 35. With Woody Allen (Harry Block), Kirstie Alley (Joan), Bob Balaban (Richard), Demi Moore (Helen), Tobey Maguire (Harvey Stern), Elisabeth Shue (Fay), Robin Williams (Mel).
• An uncompromising portrait of Harry Block, a successful writer with more than a few hidden vices.

Celebrity   1998
Screenplay Woody Allen. **Cinematography** Sven Nykvist. **Editing** Susan E. Morse. **Producers** Jean Doumanian, J. E. Beaucaire, Richard Brick, Letty Aronson (Sweetland Films), Jack Rollins and Charles H. Joffe (Rollins & Joffe Productions). **Running time** 1h 43 . With Kenneth Branagh (Lee Simon), Melanie Griffith (Nicole Oliver), Winona Ryder (Nola), Leonardo DiCaprio (Brandon Darrow), Judy Davis (Robin Simon), Joe Mantegna (Tony Cardella), Charlize Theron (Supermodel).
• A tale of life in the spotlights, from the catwalk to the film set.

Sweet and Lowdown   1999
Screenplay Woody Allen. **Cinematography** Zhao Fei. **Editing** Alisa Lepselter. **Producers** Jean Doumanian, J. E. Beaucaire, Richard Brick, Letty Aronson (Sweetland Films), Jack Rollins and Charles H. Joffe (Rollins & Joffe Productions). **Running time** 1h 35. With Sean Penn (Emmet Ray), Samantha Morton (Hattie), Uma Thurman (Blanche), Tony Darrow (Ben), Woody Allen (as himself), Constance Shulman (Hazel).
• The biography of fictional jazz guitarist Emmett Ray, an alcoholic obsessed with Django Reinhardt and torn between two women.

Small Time Crooks   2000
Screenplay Woody Allen. **Cinematography** Zhao Fei. **Editing** Alisa Lepselter. **Producers** Jean Doumanian, J. E. Beaucaire, Helen Robin, Letty Aronson (Sweetland Films and DreamWorks), Jack Rollins and Charles H. Joffe (Rollins & Joffe Productions). **Running time** 1h 35. With Woody Allen (Ray Winkler), Tracey Ullman ('Frenchy' Winkler), Hugh Grant (David), Michael Rapaport (Dennis Doyle), Jon Lovitz (Benny Borkowshi), Elaine May (May Sloan).
• An ordinary couple turn a pizzeria into a bakery as a cover for tunnelling into the bank next door. The bank job turns out to be less profitable than Frenchy's cookies and their new-found financial success allows Winkler to enter the cruel world of high society.

The Curse of the Jade Scorpion   2001
Screenplay Woody Allen. **Cinematography** Zhao Fei. **Producers** Letty Aronson, Helen Robin, Datty Ruth, Stephen Tenenbaum (DreamWorks), Charles H. Joffe (Rollins & Joffe Productions). **Running time** 1h 43. With Woody Allen (C. W. Briggs), Helen Hunt (Betty Ann Fitzgerald), Elizabeth Berkley (Jill), John Schuck (Mize), Charlize Theron (Laura Kensington).
• Insurance company investigator C. W. Briggs can't stand his new colleague, Betty Ann. But in spite of their antipathy, chance brings them together when both are hypnotized by a magician who uses them to commit a series of crimes. Their involuntary careers as criminals lead C. W. and Betty Ann to discover their true feelings for each other.

Hollywood Ending   2002
Screenplay Woody Allen. **Cinematography** Wedigo von Schultzendorff. **Editing** Alisa Lepselter.

Producers Letty Aronson, Helen Robin, Stephen Tenenbaum (Dream-Works), Jack Rollins and Charles H. Joffe (Rollins & Joffe Productions). **Running time** 1h 54. With Woody Allen (Val Waxman), Téa Leoni (Ellie), George Hamilton (Ed), Treat Williams (Hal), Debra Messing (Lori), Mark Rydell (Al), Tiffani Thiessen (Sharon Bates).
• An over-the-hill film director goes blind during the shooting of his new film.

Anything Else 2003
Screenplay Woody Allen. **Cinematography** Darius Khondji. **Editing** Alisa Lepselter. **Producers** Letty Aronson, Benny Medina, Helen Robin, Stephen Tenenbaum (DreamWorks), Jack Rollins and Charles H. Joffe. **Running time** 1h 48. With Woody Allen (David Dobel), Jason Biggs (Jerry Falk), Christina Ricci (Amanda), Stockard Channing (Paula), Danny DeVito (Harvey).
• A young New York comedian, at loggerheads with a beautiful but neurotic woman, gets some useful advice from his mentor, a writer in his sixties who is terrified by anti-Semitism.

Melinda and Melinda 2004
Screenplay Woody Allen. **Cinematography** Vilmos Zsigmond. **Editing** Alisa Lepselter. **Producers** Letty Aronson, Helen Robin, Stephen Tenenbaum (Fox Searchlight Pictures), Jack Rollins and Charles H. Joffe (Rollins & Joffe Productions). **Running time** 1h 39. With Radha Mitchell (Melinda), Will Ferrell (Hobie), Wallace Shawn (Sy), Chloë Sevigny (Laurel), Amanda Peet (Susan).
• Two friends eating at a restaurant embark on an adventure in story-telling. One tells the story of Melinda – a beautiful neurotic who crosses the path of a New York couple – as tragedy; the other tells it as comedy.

Match Point 2005
Screenplay Woody Allen. **Cinematography** Remi Adefarasin. **Editing** Alisa Lepselter. **Producers** Letty Aronson, Nicky Kentish Barnes, Lucy Darwin, Helen Robin, Stephen Tenenbaum, Gareth Wiley (BBC Films), Jack Rollins and Charles H. Joffe (Rollins & Joffe Productions). **Running time** 2h 04. With Jonathan Rhys Meyers (Chris Wilton), Scarlett Johansson (Nola Rice), Emily Mortimer (Chloe Hewett Wilton), Matthew Goode (Tom Hewett).
• Set in contemporary England, Chris is a young Irish social climber willing to use murder to defend his new position of prestige.

Scoop 2006
Screenplay Woody Allen. **Cinematography** Remi Adefarasin. **Editing** Alisa Lepselter. **Producers** Letty Aronson, Nicky Kentish Barnes, Helen Robin, Stephen Tenenbaum, Gareth Wiley (BBC Films), Charles H. Joffe and Jack Rollins (Rollins & Joffe Productions). **Running time** 1h 36. With Woody Allen (Splendini), Scarlett Johansson (Sondra Pransky), Hugh Jackman (Peter Lyman).
• A murdered reporter comes back from the dead courtesy of a magic show and reveals the identity of a serial killer to a young trainee journalist, who sets out to unmask the murderer.

Cassandra's Dream 2007
Screenplay Woody Allen. **Cinematography** Vilmos Zsigmond. **Editing** Alisa Lepselter. **Producers** Letty Aronson, Stephen Tenenbaum, Gareth Wiley. **Running time** 1h 48. With Colin Farrell (Terry), Ewan McGregor (Ian), Tom Wilkinson (Howard).
• Two brothers, one in debt and the other dreaming of becoming an investor, appeal to their super-rich uncle. He agrees to help them, if they will help him.

Vicky Cristina Barcelona 2008
Screenplay Woody Allen. **Cinematography** Javier Aguirresarobe. **Editing** Alisa Lepselter. **Producers** Letty Aronson, Stephen Tenenbaum, Gareth Wiley. **Running time** 1h 37. With Scarlett Johansson (Cristina), Rebecca Hall (Vicky), Javier Bardem (Juan Antonio), Penélope Cruz (María Elena).
• During a stay of several months in Barcelona, two young American women fall under the spell of a casanova with a highly explosive ex-wife.

Whatever Works 2009
Screenplay Woody Allen. **Cinematography** Harris Savides. **Editing** Alisa Lepselter. **Producers** Letty Aronson, Stephen Tenenbaum. **Running time** 1h 32. With Larry David (Boris Yellnikoff), Evan Rachel Wood (Melodie St. Ann Celestine), Ed Begley, Jr (John), Patricia Clarkson (Marietta), Henry Cavill (Randy James).
• In his sixties Boris Yelnikoff finds love with a girl newly arrived in New York from the Deep South.
in the sleeping compartment of the beautiful Eve Kendall.

You Will Meet a Tall Dark Stranger 2010
Screenplay Woody Allen. **Cinematography** Vilmos Zsigmond. Editing Alisa Lepselter. **Producer** Letty Aronson, Jaume Roures, Stephen Tenenbaum. **Running time** 1h 38. With Naomi Watts (Sally), Josh Brolin (Roy), Anthony Hopkins (Alfie), Antonio Banderas (Greg).
• The film revolves around different members of a family, their tangled love lives and their attempts to try to solve their problems.

Selected Bibliography

Woody Allen on Woody Allen: In Conversation with Stig Björkman (revised ed.), Grove Press, New York, 2005.

John Baxter, *Woody Allen: A Biography*, Carroll & Graf Publishers, New York, 2000.

Eric Lax, *Woody Allen: A Biography*, Da Capo Press, New York and Cambridge, MA, 2000 (first published 1991).

Marion Meade, *The Unruly Life of Woody Allen: A Biography*, Cooper Square Press, New York, 2001.

Linda Sunshine (ed.), *The Illustrated Woody Allen Reader*, Random House, New York, 1995 (first published 1993).

Notes

1. Allen has always been quick to state how much he likes Groucho Marx. The two met in the 1960s and became friends.

2. Eric Lax, *Woody Allen: A Biography*, Da Capo Press, New York and Cambridge, MA, 2000 (first published 1991), p. 19.

3. *New York Stories* (1989) consists of three sections directed by the great New York directors Martin Scorsese, Francis Ford Coppola and Woody Allen.

4. Brooklyn is the most densely populated of New York City's five boroughs.

5. A play written by Allen and performed by him on stage, then adapted for the cinema and directed by Herbert Ross in 1972, with Allen taking the leading role.

6. Marion Meade, *The Unruly Life of Woody Allen: A Biography*, Cooper Square Press, New York, 2001 33.

7. Lax, *op. cit.,* p. 18.

8. *Woody Allen on Woody Allen: In Conversation with Stig Björkman* (revised edn), Grove Press, New York, 2005, pp. 2-3.

9. For example, in *Love and Death* (1975) Allen borrows from Charlie Chaplin for the silent-film-style walk in the woods with Sonja, and from Ingmar Bergman's *Persona* (1966) when, at the end of the film, Jessica Harper's profile partly masks Diane Keaton's face.

10. Jean-Michel Frodon, *Conversation avec Woody Allen: d'après les entretiens parus dans 'Le Monde'*, Plon, Paris, 2000, p. 123.

11. Lax, *op. cit.,* p. 9.

12. John Baxter, *Woody Allen: A Biography*, Carroll & Graf Publishers, New York, 2000, p. 45.

13. *Summer with Monika* (1953) is the portrait of a free spirit and a love story that comes to a sudden end. As it contains several nude scenes, it was marketed by the American distributor as an erotic film, thus ensuring its commercial success.

14. Björkman, *op. cit.,* p. 6.

15. Mike Nichols (born 1931) was already one of the most respected theatre and film directors of the day (*Who's Afraid of Virginia Woolf?*, 1966; *The Graduate*, 1967; *Carnal Knowledge*, 1971).

16. Warren Beatty (born 1937) was to become the respected director of five films, including *Reds* (1981).

17. Suzanne Finstad, *Warren Beatty: A Private Man*, Harmony Books, New York, 2005, p. 312.

18. Finstad, *op. cit.,* p. 330. In reality, Allen never became a producer but ensured he retained total artistic control by working only with close friends or his sister, Letty Aronson.

19. Björkman, *op. cit.,* p. 10.

20. Björkman, *op. cit.,* p. 8.

21. Linda Sunshine (ed.), *The Illustrated Woody Allen Reader*, Random House, New York, 1995 (first published 1993), p. 216.

22. Sunshine, *op. cit.,* p. 52.

23. Meade, *op. cit.,* p. 74.

24. Björkman, *op. cit.,* p. 15.

25. Björkman, *op. cit.,* p. 13.

26. There are two television adaptations of *Don't Drink the Water*. The first, by Howard Morris, dates from 1969 and marks Jack Rollins and Charles H. Joffe's move into production. The second was produced by Jean Doumanian and directed by Woody Allen (1994).

27. Meade, *op. cit.,* p. 68.

28. Meade, *op. cit.,* p. 77.

29. Mickey Rose, born in Brooklyn in 1935, met Woody Allen at school. He first worked in television, then co-wrote several scripts with Allen. He continued his career in California, which makes him one source of the character played by Tony Roberts in *Annie Hall*. He worked on the television series *Happy Days* and *Charlie's Angels*, among others.

30. Ralph Rosenblum (1925–95) was a favourite editor of Sidney Lumet and Mel Brooks.

31. These were ten Hollywood figures sent to prison in 1930 for 'un-American activities'. Hollywood was a particular target of Senator Joseph McCarthy's witch-hunt against American communists, provoking terror among actors, screenwriters and directors.

32. Björkman, *op. cit.*, p. 77.

33. Björkman, *op. cit.*, p. 54.

34. In a cinema queue Alvy is annoyed by a man behind him, who is sounding off about Marshall McLuhan, the famous communications theorist and inventor of the term 'the global village'. Alvy brings in McLuhan himself, who at once appears to refute what the man is saying and pronounce Alvy correct. Alvy then addresses the audience, saying, 'Boy, if life were only like this!'

35. Woody Allen, *Getting Even*, *Without Feathers* and *Side Effects*.

36. Jean-Luc Godard's *King Lear* dates from 1987. Following a conflict between the filmmaker and his producers, the film remained unreleased until 2002. Godard was sufficiently struck by his encounter with Allen to make a short about it, *Meetin' WA* (1986), which shows a conversation between the two filmmakers intercut with drawings and paintings by Edward Hopper.

37. George Gershwin's works, from his opera *Porgy and Bess* (1935) to his concertos and two rhapsodies for solo piano and jazz orchestra, including the famous *Rhapsody in Blue* (1924), combine the great classical tradition with the modern, popular form of jazz. Woody Allen's world is in perfect harmony with this music: as a filmmaker he also combines a certain narrative classicism with an inventive modernity of form.

38. Meade, *op. cit.*, p. 117.

39. *The New York Review of Books*, 16 August 1979.

40. Lax, *op. cit.*, p. 46.

41. Meade, *op. cit.*, p. 155.

42. Björkman, *op. cit.*, p. 136.

43. Frodon, *op. cit.*, p. 165.

44. *Hannah and Her Sisters* won three Oscars: Best Supporting Actor (Michael Caine), Best Supporting Actress (Dianne Wiest) and Best Screenplay (Woody Allen).

45. The plot of *September* draws directly on a famous story from Hollywood history: the murder of Johnny Stompanato, small-time gangster and lover of Lana Turner, by Turner's daughter, Cheryl Crane, then aged fourteen.

46. Gena Rowlands acted in all the films made by her husband John Cassavetes, from *A Child is Waiting* (1963) to *Love Streams* (1984).

47. Lax, *op. cit.*, p. 363.

48. Lax, *op. cit.*, p. 311–12.

49. Over the years, most of Allen's actresses have received Oscar nominations. The exception is Mia Farrow, who has been unfairly passed over by the Academy in favour of, for example, Dianne Wiest in the year of *Hannah and Her Sisters*.

50. Björkman, *op. cit.*, p. 230–1.

51. Like that of K., the protagonist of Kafka's *The Trial*, Kleinman's life is turned upside-down overnight and threatened with destruction, with no rational explanation.

52. The precise year of Soon-Yi's birth is unknown. As a child she was mistreated by her prostitute mother before being found in an orphanage by the Previns and adopted in 1978.

53. Michael Blakemore, 'Death Defying Director', *The New Yorker*, 3 June 1996.

54. Frodon, *op. cit.*, p. 64.

55. Björkman, *op. cit.*, p. 365.

56. Woody Allen, 'Excerpts From the Spanish Diary', *The New York Times*, 20 August 2008.

Woody Allen on the set of *Broadway Danny Rose* (1984).

Sources

Collection BIFI: p.31.
Collection Cahiers du cinéma: inside front cover, pp.2–3, 6, 12–3, 15, 18–9, 20, 22, 22–3, 26, 30, 32–3, 45, 47, 48, 49, 51, 56, 57, 58–9, 61, 63, 64, 65, 66, 68, 72 (1st col.; 2nd col. bottom; 3rd col. top), 74, 78–9, 81, 82, 84–5, 86, 87, 89, 91, 93 (top), 94 (3rd and 4th col.), 95 (1st and 3rd col.), 96 (2nd col. top and bottom; 3rd col. top; 4th col. centre and bottom), 97 (2nd col. top and bottom; 3rd and 4th col.), 98 (1st col. top and bottom; 2nd, 3rd and 4th col.), 99 (1st col. top; 2nd col. top and bottom; 3rd col. top), 100–1, 103.

Collection Cahiers du cinéma/D. Rabourdin: pp.39, 43, 55, 96 (3rd col. bottom), 97 (1st col. centre).

Collection CAT'S: pp.40–1, 42, 52–3, 54, 60, 69, 70–1, 73, 75, 76–7, 83, 88, 93 (centre), 95 (4th col. bottom), 97 (1st col. bottom), 99 (1st col. bottom; 2nd col. centre; 3rd col. centre), inside back cover.

Collection Cinémathèque Française: p.96 (3rd col. centre).

Screen grabs: pp.76, 80, 84, 92.

Stig Björkman Collection: pp.24, 27, 96 (2nd col. centre).

Sun Rgia Collection: pp.4–5, 9, 38, 44, 50, 62, 72 (2nd col. top; 3rd col. bottom), 96 (4th col. top), 97 (1st col. top; 2nd col. centre).

The Kobal Collection: cover, pp.17, 28–9, 34–5, 36–7.

Credits

© American Broadcasting Company (ABC)/Jack Rollins & Charles H. Joffe Productions/Palomar Pictures International: p.27 (right).

© APJAC Productions/Paramount Pictures/Rollins-Joffe Productions: pp.27 (left), 96 (2nd col. centre).

© BBC Films/Ingenious Film Partners/Jelly Roll Productions Limited/Perdido Productions: pp.95 (4th col. bottom), 99 (2nd col. centre).

© BBC Films/Thema Production/Jada Productions Ltd./Kudu Films/Bank of Ireland/Invicta Capital: p.92 (bottom).

© BBC Films/Thema Production/Jada Productions Ltd./Kudu Films/Clive Coote: pp.89, 99 (2nd col. top).

© Cinerama/The Kobal Collection: pp.28–9.

© John Clifford: p.98 (4th col. centre).

© Columbia Pictures Corporation/Famous Artists Productions: pp.22, 22–3, 24, 96 (2nd col. top).

© Columbia Sony Pictures: pp.93 (centre), 99 (3rd col. centre).

© Columbia TriStar Films: p.98 (1st col. top).

© Columbia TriStar Pictures/Brian Hamill: pp.72 (1st col. bottom; 2nd col. top), 76–7, 80, 98 (1st col. centre).

© DreamWorks LLC/John Clifford: p.98 (4th col. bottom).

© Fox Searchlight Pictures/Perdido Productions/Brian Hamill: pp.88, 99 (1st col. bottom).

© Hallmark Entertainment/RHI Entertainment/Brian Hamill: pp.82 (top), 83, 98 (2nd col. centre).

© Brian Hamill: pp.2–3, 94 (3rd col. bottom).

© Jack Rollins & Charles H. Joffe Productions: pp.6, 18–9, 20, 30, 31, 32–3, 39, 65, 96 (2nd col. bottom; 3rd and 4th col.), 97 (3rd col. top and centre), 99 (1st col. top), 100–1, 103.

© Jack Rollins & Charles H. Joffe Productions/Brian Hamill: inside front cover, pp.4–5, 40–1, 42, 43, 44, 45, 47, 48, 49, 50, 51, 94 (3rd col. top), 97 (1st col. top).

© Jean Doumanian Productions/Cabin Creek Films/Sweetland Films: pp.76, 84 (bottom), 84–5, 87, 95 (2nd col.), 98 (2nd col. bottom; 3rd col. bottom).

© Magnolia Pictures/Miramax Films/Sweetland Films/Brian Hamill: pp.81, 82 (bottom), 98 (2nd col. top).

© Magnolia Productions Inc./Sweetland Films/Brian Hamill: pp.78–9, 98 (1st col. bottom).

© Magnolia Productions Inc./Sweetland Films/B.V.: pp.86, 95 (3rd col. top; 4th col. top).

© Orion Pictures Corporation: p.92 (top).

© Orion Pictures Corporation/Andy Schwartz: p.94 (4th col.).

© Orion Pictures Corporation/Brian Hamill: pp.9, 26, 38, 52–3, 54, 55, 56, 57, 58–9, 60, 61, 62, 63, 64, 66, 68, 69, 70–1, 72 (1st col. top; 2nd col. bottom; 3rd col.), 73, 74, 75, 97 (1st col. centre and bottom; 2nd col. 3rd col. bottom; 4th col.), inside back cover.

© Sony Pictures Classics: pp.93 (bottom), 99 (3rd col. bottom).

© Svensk Filmindustri: p.15.

© Touchstone Pictures/Brian Hamill: pp.12–3.

© Touchstone Pictures/Warner Bros Inc.: p.95 (1st col.).

© Traverso: p.95 (4th col. top and centre).

© United Artists/The Kobal Collection: cover, pp.17, 34–5, 36–7.

© Weinstein Company: pp.91, 93 (top), 99 (2nd col. bottom; 3rd col. top).

All reasonable efforts have been made to trace the copyright holders of the photographs used in this book. We apologize to anyone that we were unable to reach.

Opposite page: Woody Allen in *Husbands and Wives* (1992).
Cover: Woody Allen in *Sleeper* (1973).
Inside front cover: Woody Allen on the set of *Manhattan* (1979).
Inside back cover: *The Purple Rose of Cairo* (1985).

Cahiers du cinéma Sarl
65, rue Montmartre
75002 Paris

www.cahiersducinema.com

Revised English edition © 2010 Cahiers du cinéma Sarl
First published as *Woody Allen* © 2007 Cahiers du cinéma Sarl

ISBN 978 2 8664 2566 1

Series conceived by Claudine Paquot
Designed by Werner Jeker/Les Ateliers du nord
Translated by Trista Selous
Printed in China

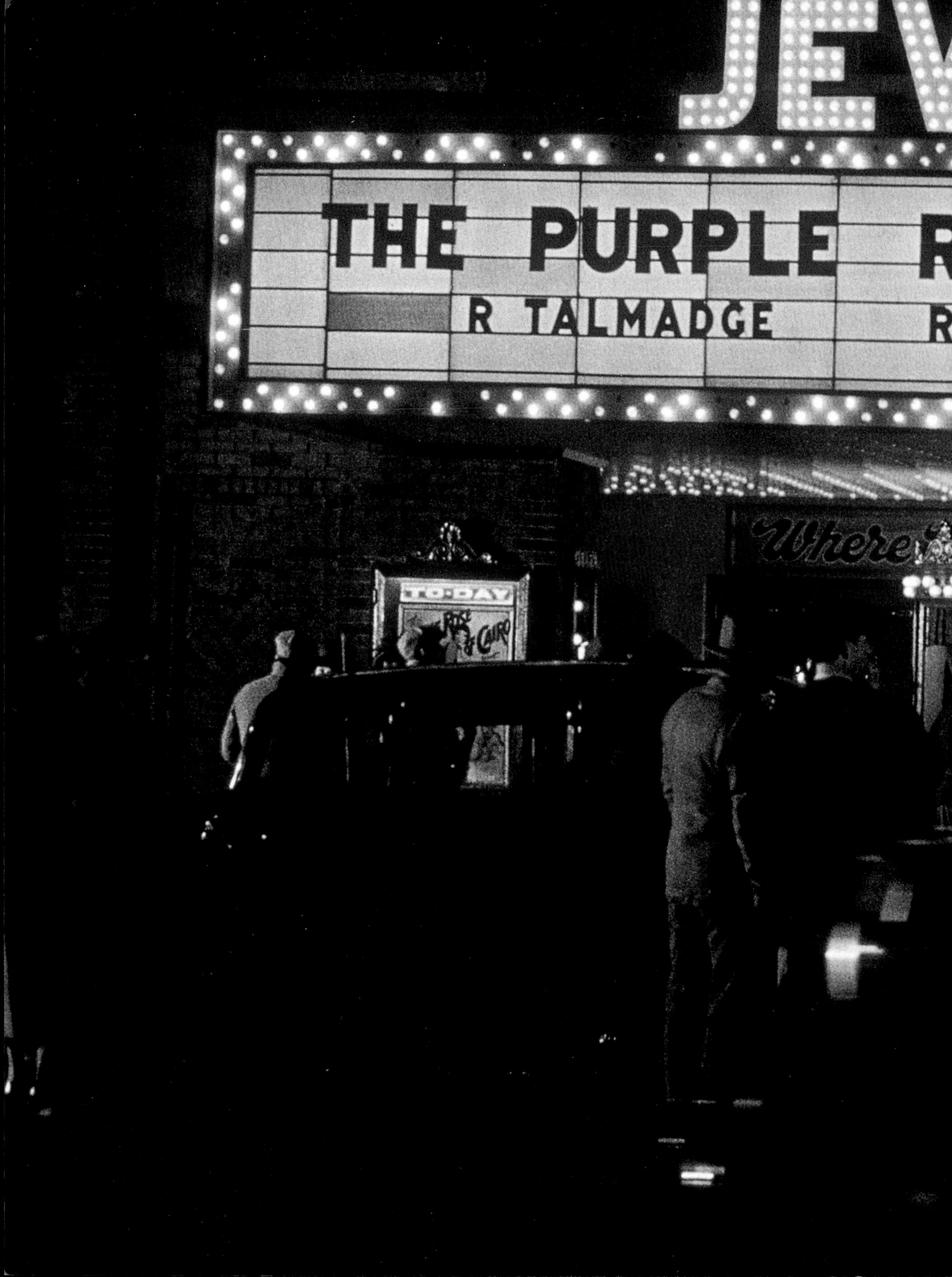
THE PURPLE
R TALMADGE
TO-DAY
Where